Melville's ISRAEL POTTER

A Pilgrimage and Progress

by

Arnold Rampersad

Bowling Green University Popular Press
Bowling Green, Ohio 43402 USA

ACKNOWLEDGMENTS

For permission to publish excerpts the author is grateful to the publishers listed below.

Charles Angoff, <u>A Literary History of the American People</u>, Tudor Publishing Company, New York, copyright 1931.

Newton Arvin, <u>Herman Melville, A Critical Biography</u>, William Sloane Associates, Inc., copyright 1950. Reprinted in paperback by Compass Books, a division of Viking Press, New York, 1957.

Morton Bloomfield, <u>Piers Plowman as a Fourteenth-Century Apocalypse</u>, Rutgers University Press, New Brunswick, New Jersey, copyright 1961.

Emilio Cecchi, "Two Notes on Herman Melville," from Agostino Lombardo, ed., <u>Italian Criticism of American Literature</u>, Mondadori Publishing Co., Milan, Italy. Quoted by permission. First publication in <u>Sewanee Review</u>. Copyright of English translation by the University of the South. Quoted by permission.

Richard M. Dorson, <u>America Rebels</u>, Pantheon Books, a Division of Random House, Inc., New York, copyright 1953. Reprinted in paperback by Fawcett World Library, New York.

F. O. Matthiessen, <u>American Renaissance</u>, Oxford University Press, New York, copyright 1941.

Library of Congress Catalogue Number 71-79980

© Copyright 1969 by the Bowling Green University Popular Press. All rights reserved. Printed in the United States of America.

PS 2384 .I73 R3 1969
813 M497ra

Rampersad, Arnold.

Melville's Israel Potter

For Herschell and Barbara Lewis

IN GRATITUDE

With the soul of an Atheist, he wrote down the Godliest things; with the feeling of misery and death in him, he created forms of gladness and life.

<u>Pierre</u> (Bk. XXV, Ch. iii)

Melville's ISRAEL POTTER

A Pilgrimage and Progress

CONTENTS

Introduction		i
Preface		vii
Chapter I	The Wake of the Whale	1
Chapter II	Old Tombstone Retouched	16
Chapter III	The Monthly Melville	45
Chapter IV	Broadcloth and Linsey-Woolsey	67
Chapter V	Harpoon into Plowshare	86
Chapter VI	Requiescat in Pace	107
Notes		118
Bibliography		127

INTRODUCTION

Popular art suffers today from comparison with sophisticated--or elite--art and with folk art. To a certain extent, of course, this derogation of popular art is justifiable, but to a considerable degree it is the direct consequence of misunderstanding and snobbery.

The growth of popular art should be seen in its historical development. Up to the eighteenth century there was essentially no such thing, or no labeling as such. There were only folk art and sophisticated art, and they were closely allied, at times, indeed, virtually overlays one of the other. With the democratic impulses of the eighteenth century, however, the gap between sophisticated art and folk art became more real, and widened. Until this century the only distinction between "folk" art and "popular" art, between the "folk" and their "popular" counterparts, was that between rural and urban. The lives led by both groups of people--and the art they created--was essentially the same. With the growth of the masses during the eighteenth century the schism between the folk and the other people widened. The momentum of the spread accelerated, but by the middle and end of the nineteenth century often the difference was not real or was ignored. Abraham Lincoln, for example, in the middle of the century still lived in the world of both and did not distinguish between them. Even Mark Twain, later--perhaps more sharply aware of the two than many of his contemporaries--moved from one to the other without apparent motion sickness.

The development of the mass media of communication in the middle of the twentieth century, however, has driven larger wedges between folk art and popular art and between popular art and elite art, or so many critics these days like to think, and caused the general blanket condemnation of popular art which existed in this century up until the last decade.

Such influential elitist critics of our culture as Dwight Macdonald and Edmund Wilson have always insisted that whatever was widespread was artistically and esthetically deficient, therefore unworthy of study. They taught that only the elite, the aristocratic and minority can produce real art. Excepting folk art, which they recognized as sometimes reaching high esthetic standards, they insisted that mass or popular art was an abomination, a sell-out by unprincipled hucksters to the desire to make a fast buck, and a vitiation of high culture and high art. This attitude, unhappily, persists today among some of the younger critics. William Gass, for example, a creative writer of considerable force, insists that popular art is devoid of all esthetic quality.

Increasingly these days, however, the battery of critical guns being fired against the bastions of prejudice and snobbery is being increased in number and fire power. Such an observant young author as Tom Wolfe, perhaps writing more viscerally than intellectually, thumbs his nose at the elitist critics who insist that anything "mass" is necessarily specious and unesthetic. Even more compellingly the brilliant young critic and esthetician Susan Sontag bludgeons the old point of view. Far from alarmed at the apparent new esthetic--or lack of any--she sees that new liberties in accepting much of the new products of popular culture are merely a change in attitude, not a death's blow to culture and art. To her art today is a "new kind of instrument," and the complexity of the present-day world made this change in attitude toward art and in art inevitable. She insists that the distinction between elite and popular art(the preachments of Matthew Arnold, the high priest of the elitist critics, not withstanding) seem "less and less meaningful." It is important to emphasize, as she does, that this increased concern with popular art is "not a new phili--
tinism." The changed attitude merely demonstrates that increasingly artists and critics--and many others--are merely opening their eyes to the world they live in.

More and more these days critics recognize that there are several levels of art in the broad vertical spectrum and varying degrees of success and failure in esthetic accomplishment in all. With more brevity and wit than truth critics in the past have classified the levels as High-Brow, Mid-Brow and Low-Brow, apparently leaving out that level that would perhaps best be called Folk-Brow. But nobody ought seriously to contend that there are not some differences of accomplishment in each level. Nobody could affirm that all of Shakespeare's plays are of equal merit, all of Wordsworth's poems pure gold, some of Faulkner's works not inferior to others, and even some of Mozart's works more meritorious than others. These "elite" artists were serious in their approach to their work.

In general the serious artists value individualism, individual expression, the exploration and discovery of new depths in life's experiences.

On the popular level there is less emphasis placed upon, and less accomplishment reached in, this plumbing of reality. Generally speaking popular and mass artists are less interested in the experimental and searching than in the restatement of the old and accepted. But it should never be denied that there are actually vast differences in the esthetic achievements attained in the works from these two levels, and different aspirations and goals, even within these somewhat limited objectives.

The popular artist is usually much superior to the mass artist. The former does not accept the formulas, the sterotypes, merely as frames on which to stretch his used and faded canvases. He changes his material through reorganization, selection and stress. His goal is in fact "recreation." The mass artist, on the other hand, sticks strictly to the formula. Instead of recharging the experience with his own recreation, he decharges the potential by simplifying, building on stock experiences and seeking stock responses. No better distinction between the two can be found than between the banjo player Johnny St. Cyr and Liberace. St. Cyr always responded to his stimulus with the fire of spontaneous creation. When his audience was enthusiastic, he played with more and more spirit, creating and never playing the same tune twice. Liberace, on the other hand, admits that he is concerned with the threshold of acceptance of his audience. He reads them, and plays exactly what, like the automobile designer, he thinks they want.

St. Cyr is a truly creative artist both in intent and accomplishment. His credentials are not invalidated merely by the fact that he works in essentially a popular idiom. Given the limitations of his medium--if indeed these limitations are real-- he can still be just as great a creator as--perhaps greater than-- Rubenstein. It is unfair to pit jazz against classical music, the popular artist against the elite artist. They are not in competition. Each has its own purposes, techniques and accomplishments. They complement each other rather than compete.

It is also unfair to give blanket condemnation to mass art though obviously the accomplishments of mass art are much less than those of other forms. Liberace does not aspire to much and perhaps reaches even less. His purposes and techniques are inferior, but not all of his accomplishments, or those of the many other workers on his level, are completely without value.

Popular art also includes folk art, an element that we have so far not sufficiently discussed. The relationship between folk art and popular art and between folk art and elite art is still debatable. In many ways folk art borrows from and imitates both.

Historically folk art has come more from the hall than from the hovel, has depended more upon the truly creative-- though unsophisticated--spirit than the mediocre imitator. "Sir Patrick Spens," one of the greatest songs (poems) ever written, was originally the product of a single creative genius. Today's best folklore-to-be, that is the most esthetically satisfying folklore that is working into tradition today, is that of the powerful individual artist such as Woody Guthrie and Larry Gorman.

To a disappointingly large number of observers, however, folklore is felt to be the same as popular culture, and folk art derives directly from popular art, with only a slight time lag. To such critics, today's popular art is tomorrow's folk art. Both notions are gross and out of line.

Esthetically folk art has two levels. There is superb folk art and deficient, mediocre folk art. Generally folk art, despite the lack of sophistication much of it has, is more nearly akin to elite art than to popular art. In motivation of artist, also, folk art is close to elite, for like the elite artist the truly accomplished folk artist values individualism and personal expression, he explores new forms and seeks new depths in expression and feeling. But there are at the same time many workers in folk art who are mere imitators, just trying to get along-- exactly like their counterparts in mass art.

Thus all levels in artistic accomplishment are closely related and not mutually exclusive one from another. They constitute one long continuum. Perhaps the best metaphorical figure for all is that of a flattened ellipsis, or a lens. In the center, largest in bulk and easiest seen through is popular art, which includes mass art. On either end of the lens are high and folk art, both looking fundamentally alike in many respects and both having a great deal in common, for both have keen direct vision and extensive peripheral insight and acumen. All four derive in many ways and to many degrees from one another, and the lines of demarcation between any two are indistinct and fluid.

A sane attitude that is becoming increasingly acceptable is that held by the philosopher Abraham Kaplan--that popular art has considerable accomplishment and even more real possibilities; it is developing but has not realized its full potential.

Another of popular art's unrealized potentials-- and a revelation of its weakness--lies in what can happen when a superior artist takes the crude and uncompleted accomplishments of an inferior popular artisan and with the alchemical magic of his genius transmute base metal into gold. An excellent case in point is the ineffectual narration by Israel Potter of his mis- adventured life which Melville took and, boiling it in the try-works of his fiery genius, converted into powerful art. All of Melville's works exhibit this method and this magic. All aspects of art-- and of life--were sources of blubber for his boiling. Nothing was too lowly and mean--neither Transcendentalism, demonism, popular theater, the shanghai gesture, jokes about pills and gas on the stomach, nor any other. All were clay for bricks that he would fashion with which to build his towering mansions.

The story of Melville's accomplishment and the methods he used to achieve it is a fascinating tale which only recently has started to unfold. As yet it is only a half-told tale. Every effort to flesh out and extend the story is welcome. It is for this reason that Mr. Rampersad's study of the conversion of Israel Potter's mediocre <u>Life and Remarkable Adventures</u> into the masterful <u>Israel Potter</u> of Herman Melville is an enlightening and welcome addition to the literature of popular art in general and to the criticism of Melville in particular.

Ray B. Browne

PREFACE

In the years immediately following Moby Dick and Pierre, Herman Melville found himself struggling for survival as artist and as individual. Moby Dick, his work of genius, had been generally ignored; Pierre, a cry from the soul, had been savagely rebuffed. His moral standards, his artistic taste and his critical acumen were being attacked, and his future seemed to promise little. It is uncertain whether Melville ever considered deserting the literary profession into which he had practically stumbled but to which he had wholly committed himself; when he did write again, however, it was with great caution, and in the comparative safety of the literary magazines. That caution invaded his craft: he produced the desolate Encantadas, the enigmatic Bartleby the Scrivener and the apparently superficial Israel Potter.

Little has been written about Israel Potter; practically untouched by critical hands, the work has not received the extensive revaluation accorded Melville's major works in the twentieth century. The first fifty years brought one recorded scholarly review of Melville's methods and achievements in the novel; there are still fewer than a dozen articles at the disposal of the Melville reader. This neglect is undeserved.

Israel Potter illuminates one of the darkest passages of Melville's life, one that fostered a fundamental change in his personal and artistic philosophy. Never again would he return to the pursuit of heroic idealism that reached its apex in Moby Dick; thereafter, his concern would be with other issues: those of appearance and reality, absolutes and expediency, duty and resignation. A close examination of Israel Potter shows Melville in transition, resisting the lure of pure adventure, concerning himself with questions of national and personal identity.

There is adventure in the novel, but Melville so deploys characters and circumstances that we are soon persuaded that what is being offered is more than adventure; there are satire and burlesque to divert the reader, but Melville is too aware of the responsibilities of authorship to avoid that background of blackness which he so admired in Shakespeare and in Hawthorne, and out of which fundamental truths derived. As in any challenging work of art, there are several aspects to be considered; it is a mistake to conclude that Israel Potter is either adventure or satire without a proper examination of the novel's texture.

This study proposes such an examination. I hope to show that Melville records in Israel Potter his views on the character and future of the American nation, on the possibilities of response by individuals to the vicissitudes of life, and on the personal dilemmas that plagued Melville's existence and threatened his future as artist and provider. For what this novel reveals about Herman Melville, his life and art, it deserves a more honored place in the Melville canon, and, most certainly, greater critical attention.

I wish to record here my debt to several persons who have contributed in various ways to this study: to Professors Alma J. Payne and J. Robert Bashore, for their skill and enthusiasm in introducing me to the broad areas of American letters; to Professor Virginia E. Leland for her sensitive discussion of the varieties of symbol and allegory in the medieval setting, from which I drew conclusions about Melville's work for which she is not accountable; to Professor Ray B. Browne, who suggested several wise changes in the manuscript and who was responsible for having this work published. My greatest debt is to Professor John J. Gross, who guided me originally through the Melville library and suggested that a study of Israel Potter could provide further insight into Melville as man and artist;

Professor Gross' rich knowledge of Melville and Melville scholarship and his kindness and encouragement have been invaluable to me.

So few studies have been devoted exclusively to Israel Potter that I have found it easy to list virtually all in a short selective bibliography, together with the works of some other commentators who have sought to do justice to Melville's basis artistic integrity in his writing of Israel Potter. W. D. Jones' dissertation, the only one centering on this particular work, though it antedates my study by some four years and though it feels after insights and developments, I found generally not of any great value or use. Professor David E. Smith's John Bunyan in America (Bloomington, 1966) had little to do with Melville directly but I found it especially valuable as a guide to an important allegorical process used during the American Renaissance.

Bowling Green, Ohio   A. R.
February 1969

Chapter One

The Wake of the Whale

Yankee pedlars roving through New England and beyond late in 1824 might have taken with them a few copies of a thin volume of remarkable adventures allegedly written by one Israel R. Potter, a native of Cranston in Rhode Island.[1] Sales of the book must have been encouraging. Two printers issued it from their Providence presses in the home state of the author;[2] perhaps potential buyers had already heard of the old man who had returned to the United States after almost half a century in England, only to be rejected in his petition for a pension based on his part in the War of Independence. He had fought at Bunker Hill against the British, served as a courier to Benjamin Franklin in France, and after the war had found it financially impossible to return to the country of his birth. Only in his seventy-ninth year did he finally make the voyage home, to be rebuffed in his petition and his hopes for financial security in his old age and on his native soil. In desperation, it seemed, he had turned to print to plead his cause.

Two printings testify to the persuasiveness of the tale; at about thirty cents a copy, the book must have brought some remuneration to the veteran.[3] Yet it had all but faded from the literary scene when, in the fall of 1849, young Herman Melville acquired a copy of Life and Remarkable Adventures.[4] Redburn and Whitejacket had just been written in the summer of that year; further behind Melville as author lay Typee and Omoo, the first outpouring of his craft, and the vauntingly ambitious Mardi. Apparently the work seemed at once attractive and potential material for the hard-writing Melville, for in December of the same year, in London to see his publishers, among other matters, Melville noted in his journal his plans for reworking the story:

> Looked over a lot of ancient maps of London. Bought one (A.D. 1766) for 3 & 6 pence. I want to use it in case I serve up the Revolutionary narrative of the beggar. . . .[5]

The decision whether to "serve up" the narrative of the beggar was not made easily, for there were other ideas in Melville's teeming mind and imagination as 1850 came and went. But in the summer of that year Melville was still thinking of Israel Potter as he read a newly-bought copy of A History of the County of Berkshire, Massachusetts that told of the events leading up to the battle of Lexington, the news of which had sent the real Israel Potter hastening towards Bunker Hill:

> The very year in which the first convention was held, two regiments of minute men were raised by voluntary enlistment . . . These regiments marched, immediately after the battle of Lexington, to the vicinity of Boston, where they were reorganized and enlarged. . . . Lexington battle was fought on the 18th of April, 1775; news of it arrived in Berkshire on the 20th, about noon, and the next morning at sunrise the regiment of Col. Patterson were on their way.[6]

Melville noted on the back fly-leaf of the History the pagination of these remarks, adding "Old man-soldier," in clear reference to Israel Potter, a minute-man himself in those early days of revolution.[7]

But whatever his intentions at the precise middle of the century, Melville did not then turn finally and with full concentration towards the story of Israel Potter. If Mardi had failed to captivate the critics, Redburn and Whitejacket, even though Melville could refer to them as pot-boilers, "two 'jobs' which I have done for money--being forced to it, as other men are to sawing wood,"[8] had been written with such facility and had been so well received that Melville clearly felt himself at a high creative point, equipped at last to deal with the metaphysical abstractions and the attendant problems of symbolism, imagery, theme, characterisation and plot that had collapsed under stress in the pages of Mardi. There was a tale of a great white whale to be told, and of a demoniacal captain and his cosmopolite crew who sailed the world in pursuit of that whale to their ultimate destruction, as well as of a too-sensitive and idealistic young man acting neither wisely nor too well, drawing upon himself and his women the wrath of an offended social order. The remarkable adventures must have appeared small stuff next to such presences; the book was not written until Melville had known personal and literary disaster.

The details of that disaster have become commonplaces of Melville biography; it is accepted that the years after the publication of Moby Dick and Pierre represented an ordeal of the most injurious kind for Herman Melville. Yet it is important for this study, which attempts in part to see Israel Potter as representing a major rehabilitative step of great importance to the author, that aspects of those years should be highlighted. It is even more important that the impact of failure on Melville's fundamental literary beliefs, and the resultant modifications imposed on his craft in response to failure, be examined. For Israel Potter, properly examined, indicates the resilience of Melville as a writer, his appreciation of the tradition of English literature into which he was born, his own severe self-critical faculties, and the proof of his courage and ability to resist nihilism and rejection.

> Israel Potter well merits the present tribute--a private of Bunker Hill, who for his faithful services was years ago promoted to a still deeper privacy under the ground, with a post-humous pension, in default of any during life, annually paid him by the spring in ever new mosses and sward.[9]

It was in this spirit that Melville dedicated his new work "To his Highness, the Bunker Hill Monument." Moby Dick had been dedicated to Nathaniel Hawthorne, but Pierre was inscribed to "Greylock's Most Excellent Majesty." Matthiessen found the Pierre dedication "playful rather than misanthropic";[10] the truth probably lies in a combination of both attitudes, with Melville leaning well towards the latter by the time he started Israel Potter. Israel Potter, the character, was perhaps in some ways too close to Melville's own life and experience at that time for any other inclination.

These dedications to a mountain and a monument, followed by the Confidence-Man, which was apparently dedicated to no one at all, reflected Melville's growing despair at ever communicating effectively with his potential audience; we must not infer from this, however, that Melville was at the same time growing careless about his art. In any event, Moby Dick, appreciated by a few, had been a popular failure; Pierre had received a shattering reception. The London Athenaeum had called Moby Dick "so much trash belonging to the worst school of Bedlam literature."[11] The Literary World had found Pierre "immoral"[12] and the Southern Quarterly Review thought Melville quite mad.[13] Putnam's, which was to eventually publish Israel Potter, wrote of Melville's "inexcusable insanity,"[14] while the American Whig Review denounced the book's "repulsive, unnatural and indecent plot, . . . and ideas unparalleled for earnest absurdity."[15] Hawthorne, laconic but not uncritical, later found evidence in Melville's writings of "a morbid state of mind."[16]

It was clearly the lowest point of Melville's active career. It was what eventually moved Maria Melville to write to Peter Gansevoort in April of 1853 that "Herman would be greatly benefited by a sojourn abroad, he would then be compelled to more intercourse with his fellow creatures. It would very materially renew, and strengthen both his body and mind."[17] The sojourn abroad hopefully was to be at the expense of the United States government, which under President Pierce had evinced a new interest in rewarding distinguished American artists. Melville's attempt to secure a consulship, almost any consulship, was supported by Hawthorne, Amasa Parker, G.Y. Lansing, Charles O'Connor, Edward C. West and Edwin and Sherman Croswell, as well as Caleb Cushing, Phineas Allen Jr. and James L. Buren.[18] Arvin writes :

> Taken together, they must have had the air of a powerful group of backers; but they accomplished nothing. Melville, no doubt, had held himself too completely aloof from politics; he had put no man a penny in his debt, Whig or Democrat; and then, too,there must have been, especially after Pierre, an ill-defined but damaging impression that he was not a man whose soundness and discretion could be counted on.[19]

This must have been a blow to Melville of a particular sort, and one that made Israel's claim of service to his country, and his eventual denial of a pension on what he interpreted as a legal technicality, particularly relevant to Herman Melville. Melville had fought valiantly on behalf of American national literature both polemically, as in his review of Hawthorne's Mosses, and also by example, as in his own creations. And he, like Israel Potter, had been rejected both by the people and by the machinery of government.

And not only had Melville "put no man a penny in his debt"; his own financial indebtedness seemed to mock his literary career. We are reminded that "although he had by 1853 published seven books, he still was in debt to Harper and Brothers for seven hundred dollars in advance royalties."[20] The situation was not helped by the fire at Harper's that year, which not only destroyed stock of his work, but also financially weakened the publishing house on which he depended. "These contretemps," Von Hagen writes, "brought Melville to the resolve to leave the world of letters."[21] It was the failure of the consulship attempt that finally sent him back to the pen through the periodicals of the day, "and in that mood [he] turned to draft the Encantadas and shift his thoughts to those lugubrious, volcanic islands six hundred miles off the coast of South America."[22]

It is in this turning from personal failure to pen and paper that Melville revealed the caliber of his mind and art. This turning, at the same time, has given rise to the questionable conclusion that because Melville had been rejected he had himself begun to reject his artistic responsibilities, lowering his sights from the higher objectives to more pedestrian themes. Matthiessen talked of Melville writing under a kind of miserable compulsion, his vision blinded by his own tragedy:

> When he [Melville] came to the ex-soldier's destitution in London, his own sense of suffering was so great that he could not bear to dwell on Potter's, and slurred over what was to have been his main subject in a couple of short chapters.[23]

Newton Arvin, too, found Melville faltering in the years after *Pierre*, a writer cowering under the psychological buffeting that had come with practically each review and each set back:

> During the two or three years that follow, Melville has the air of consciously sparing himself; sparing himself by attempting only short and unexacting flights or by leaning heavily on some bookish source, some old volume of voyages or "remarkable adventures."[24]

This is only part of the story. It bespeaks a negative attitude towards not only Melville's skill as craftsman but also the temper of his mind, an attitude not supported by the quality of the writing that Melville produced in the years after *Pierre*. No one can ignore the defeat of *Moby Dick* or the disaster of *Pierre*, the disappointment of the Hawthorne relationship, the rejection of the consulship, the financial indebtedness, the long hours of solitary reading, the weakening health and signs of mental instability. In fact, particularly where his actual literary output was concerned, Melville could not have ignored the indisputable evidence of his errors. Re-reading *Pierre*, Melville must have observed in that passion-generated novel a veritable catalogue of his literary sins. The critical mistake lies in forgetting that Melville had been through exactly this once before, in the failure of the bombastic *Mardi*, and that he had pulled himself off the floor to fight again. This is precisely what he did after *Pierre*, and far from being the scratchings of a faltering pen, the writing between *Pierre* and the *Confidence-Man* shows Melville most firmly in command, exercising spartan discipline over his art, a creative indictment of the excesses of *Pierre*, a positive re-assessment of the whole inventory of symbolism and imagery, theme and structure, in the world of Melville's imagination.

The major question that Melville must have asked himself is the simplest: where had he gone wrong as a writer ? Sometime during that dynamic period when he had felt, he said, the need for fifty hard-writing young men to tap the resources of his mind and expose them to the world on paper, he had lost control of art, had surrendered to indiscretion, to lack of judgment. In the heat of prolonged intercourse with the imagination, the relationship had been subverted and Melville had been mastered when he had thought himself master. To understand the achievement of Israel Potter, to appreciate better why it is proably second only to Moby Dick as a complete and accomplished work of art in the Melville canon, one has necessarily to set it beside Pierre and see how it succeeds precisely where Pierre fails.

The key to Pierre's failure is its lack of adequate motivation; far from being too close to Melville, as it is so often claimed, the book is so far from Melville's own experience, vicarious or otherwise, that Melville consistently has to return to the most time-abused portrayals and situations to rescue any semblance of authenticity. He set out to write a domestic tragedy, and he set out to write it for little other reason than that it was there, and had not been done by him before. He had stated that he did not want to go down in history as the man who had lived among the savages; he might have foreseen that even today one hears of Moby Dick as one of the greatest "sea-stories" ever written. Moreover, it may be conjectured, for the relationship between the two men was then at its high point, that Melville wanted to walk the same road with Hawthorne in a kind of imitative exercise that would bring his own unique literary gifts to bear on the matters that most engaged Hawthorne as writer: the questions of ancestry and sin, of repressive psychological tyrannies and personal rebellions, of flights from and into reality. Compare Zenobia with Mrs. Glendinning, the Pyncheon portrait with the Pierre portrait, the flight from the seven-gabled house with the flight of Pierre and his sad party to the city; the whole background of darkness which Melville admired in Hawthorne and against which, he felt, Hawthorne so felicitously was able to display piercing philosophical observations, we find attempted in Pierre; unfortunately for Melville, in Pierre it is a second hand curtain bought from a neo-Gothic shop. Melville had simply not done his homework, not apprenticed himself in any craft other than the modified epic form so suited to tales of the sea.

It was a major blunder, one of the few that Melville ever

made in reconciling his individual talent to the great tradition of English literature stretching from Beowulf to his own day. Far more than any other American writer of the century, and even in the face of his protestation of American autonomy in art, Melville felt free, if not obliged, to draw from the masterworks of European literature. He knew precisely what had succeeded and what had not in the making of the great masterpieces that he admired. Matthiessen, for one, has amply traced the origins of that "bold and nervous lofty language,"[25] compiling the list of Melville's debts to Thomas Browne and Shakespeare, to Milton and the Bible, to Dante and Rabelais and, in his own time, to Carlyle. With this there is obvious in Melville a determination to write the great book, a hunger after recognition, more than mere excellence, that we do not find in Hawthorne. It undoubtedly resulted from Melville's highly unstructured education; there is the pride of the self-made man in Melville's note that a whaling ship had been his Harvard and his Yale, but there is a concomitant note of regret confirmed when we know that Melville admitted to not really having known the work of Shakespeare until he was twenty-five. He is close to autobiography in Pierre when he writes that

> Pierre was resolved to give the world a book, which the world would hail with surprise and delight. A varied scope of reading, little suspected by his friends, and randomly acquired by a random and lynx-eyed mind, in the course of the multifarious, incidental, bibliographic encounterings of almost any civilized young enquirer after truth; this poured one considerable contributory stream into that bottomless spring of original thought which the occasion and time had caused to burst out in himself (Bk. XXI, Chapter i).

On one hand, this is a description of an intellectual nouveau riche; on the other, it tells the story of Melville's perennial literary eclecticism. Melville as a writer sat directly at the feet of his masters, a position which few other major Americans of his time would have dared take. If Whitman wrote poetry as if no one had ever written poetry before, the more appropriate comment concerning Melville would be that attributed to Gertrude

Stein about Hemingway, that his work smelled of museums. At his writing desk, Melville was not ever primarily an American, but an heir to the tradition of all letters. This was no guarantee of success; in Pierre, with Hamlet close by, Melville was to discover that a Shakespearean flavor was simply not enough.

Having walked long on the rolling decks of whaling vessels or men-of-war, Melville had never practised the art of domestic strolling, much less the posturing and strutting of the high-fashioned Glendinning home. Indeed, Melville's bailiwick is not the whole ocean; he has favorite haunts where he rises to the high marks of his career. One perceptive Italian critic, Emilio Cecchi, has noted Melville's partiality:

> The natural setting of Melville's imagination is the Pacific (or the "Pacific of the mind") and when he sails toward other oceans or takes refuge in other seas, it is a fact to be taken into account. "Pacific" and "Atlantic" are more than mere geographical divisions--I might call them metaphysical and moral entities.[26]

From this he concludes:

> Certainly every time Melville turned his back on those prophetic shores and waters, his imagination plays in a minor key. From cosmic symbols, metaphysical intimations and the invention of new mythologies, the most noble and authentic in modern times, he passes to a historical or anecdotal world, on which his pessimism and nihilism have such a rapid and furiously destructive power, that the material of his art seems to break up and scatter at the very instant that it takes on form and color.[27]

What is true of the shift from ocean to ocean is even more remarkable in the shift from sea to land. If Melville's natural setting was the Pacific, he was at least fairly comfortable where-ever there was salt water under him, and as critics have said, uncomfortable on land. Land, as in the initiation of Redburn or with the attractiveness of Fayaway, might be a nice place to visit; Melville clearly did not wish to live there. Pierre cries near the end of the novel:

> I have sat on earth's saddle till I am weary; I must now vault over to the other saddle awhile. Oh, seems to me, there should be two ceaseless steeds for a bold man to ride,--the Land and the Sea; and like circus-men we should never dismount, but only be steadied and rested by leaping from one to the other, while still, side by side, they both race round the sun. I have been on the Land steed so long, oh I am dizzy! (Book XXVI, Chapter i)

Melville had indeed grown dizzy by the time Pierre was at an end; he had come to write this tale of family, fiancée, incest and revenge with few tools and no personal experience in writing anything like this. Remove Fayaway and the other Gauguinesque ladies of the Pacific night and Melville's work till Pierre is woman-less, a place where men share beds, with women hardly acknowledged. But, and of prime significance, Melville had honed all his weapons for the heroic tale; a shipload of men was an Anarcharsis Cloots delegation of all humanity, masts were symbols of the Holy Cross and a man plunged after a whale as he would at his God. All this had reached its apotheosis in Moby Dick, and when Ahab in his last words intones "Thus, I give up the spear," Melville is simultaneously announcing the end of the heroic road, the surrender of the spear, which, in its various forms of lance, sword or harpoon, is the principal symbol of that heroic world of Ulysses, Aeneas, Beowulf, Arthur, Roland, Ahab et alia.

One symbol--royalism or nobility--suffices to show how skilled Melville is in manipulating the threads of the heroic or epic pattern and how clumsily he attempts to manipulate the same core symbol to suit different ends in the homely tragedy of Pierre; later on, that skill returns in Israel Potter when Melville applies new standards of discrimination to his selection of symbol. While Melville worked in the area of the heroic, the royal metaphor is of extreme importance. The tradition is older than Aristotle that a great tragic hero must also be a man of elevated station in life; it took at least twenty centuries of accumulated symbolic import to create an errant salesman with genuine tragic proportions. Melville was aware of this tradition, he was aware too of a fundamental symbolic contradiction facing the urgently democratic American writers for whom kings and royal courts should have been a thing of the long colonial past, as indeed they were.

But such had been Melville's personal life experience and literary growth that his grand work (and there can be no question that he also conceived Moby Dick as a Great Work) had to be staged on the rolling and confined decks of the Pequod. It is impossible now for any literate person to view whale-hunting as less than novel, as the very stuff of the epic tradition. It is, of course, nothing of the kind without our remembrance of Moby Dick; before the appearance of the novel, whale-hunting appeared epic to few and repugnant to many. Ignorance of this primarily American industry accounts to a large extent for Melville's choosing it as a subject and for his cramming into it so much cetology. Melville was faced with this same basic contradiction in his quest after greatness: he had to create protagonist and antagonist of living epic proportion, deserving of places in the world of exalted action literature, and these would have to exist in an epic world that could, by its grandeur and scale, support the weight of that literary bombast which is the superstructure of epic.

It is important to note how Melville raises, with remarkable craft, this lowly captain to an exalted level. There is the choice of the name, Ahab: Ahab of the Bible "did more to provoke the Lord God of Israel to anger than all the kings of Israel that went before him." There the resemblance begins and ends, as far as historicity is concerned, but it is enough for Melville. The captain of a ship, as Ahab bragged, is more than king of a ship, and Ahab is made to be more than king; but in Melville's accretive creative process, Ahab is first a king. The Pequod is kingly: "Her mast stood stiffly up like the spines of the three old kings of Cologne." Queequeg is son of a king, " this sea Prince of Wales." And this prince's captain is also a king: "He's a grand, ungodly, god-like man, he's Ahab, boy, ... and Ahab of old, thou knowest, was a crowned king" (Ch. XVI).

These three observations of regalness, careful strokes of Melville, mark the rising tenor of the book. Father Mapple's sermon is stimulating and ultimately prophetic, but it is not as important to the scale of the book as these three incipient leaveners. Scale and dimension are Melville's main problems as the voyage begins, and in spite of the cloaking of those chapters on cetology in a mock-pedantic humor, charmingly exasperating, there is a sense of urgency on the writer's part to convince us that his extracts, gathered from dusty tomes by a sub-sub-librarian, still contain great truths born in Genesis.

Moby Dick, the whale antagonist of Ahab the king, must be a worthy antagonist. He, too, must be kingly, and not exclusively so in size. To lessen the potential of the whale is to lessen our involvement with Ahab and the impact of the tale. Achilles must have his Hector, and Moby Dick must have pedigree, pomp and circumstance. As the Pequod slips to sea (Ch. XXIV) Melville reminds us that "whaling is imperial! By old English statutory law, the whale is declared a 'royal fish'," and the writer postscribes that whale's supply "kings and queens with coronation stuff." The next chapter finds Melville protracting the metaphor; the mates and harpooners are "knights and squires."

Melville never forgets that the ideological and personality implications of Ahab's kingship are potentially dangerous; that kingship is a dramatic device at root, a critical judgment of the profoundly egalitarian Melville. Melville is anxious that we do not extrapolate from the royal metaphor to assumptions either that Ahab is a tyrant or pompously affected, (for Ahab is, apart from his grand obsession, little more than a stern old man, with an old salt's eccentricities) or that Melville himself is ready to compromise his democratic ideals. He interrupts his first chapter on Knights and Squires to declare his manifesto of democracy:

> But this august dignity I treat of is not the dignity of Kings and robes, but that abounding dignity that has no robed investiture . . . If, then, to meanest mariners, and renegades and castaways, I shall hereafter ascribe high qualities, . . . then against all mortal critics bear me out in it, thou just Spirit of Equality, which hast spread one royal mantle of humanity over all my king (Chap. XXVI).

The Wake of the Whale 13

Here is a totally aware Melville. Checks and balances are flawlessly deployed. Having carefully stated his intentions, Melville can move further in the elevation of Ahab to poet-king, priest-king, Christ-king. When Ahab usurps the powers of Godship in forging a harpoon out of twelve strands (with one Judas strand to be reworked), Melville resorts to the royal metaphor to announce the sealing of his fate in a scene of remarkable subtlety, where a hawk removes Ahab's hat and drops it into the sea (Chap. CXXX). Melville tells us that Tarquin (Lucius Tarquinius Priscus) had become king of Rome after a similar incident, though it was thought significant that the bird, an eagle, had returned the cap to Tarquin's head. What Melville evokes here is the memory of the history of that legendary family: Servius Tullius, successor of Lucius Tarquinius Priscus, was assassinated by Priscus' son (or grandson), Tarquin the Proud (Lucius Tarquinius Superbus); Tarquin the Proud was himself banished from the city of Rome, the last king to rule over its people. What Melville has foreshadowed in Ahab's incident is the coming disaster and dethronement of King Ahab; he eventually dies by hanging, the punishment of a common criminal.

    This particular kind of display of skill does not appear in Melville again in any sustained piece of writing until he began his reworking of Israel Potter's story. Compare what has been observed in Moby Dick with Melville's handling of symbol in Pierre and we see the transparent in domination. There are elements of the same royal metaphor invoked, the same attempt to assert the democratic spirit, but there is no similarity in effect. Pierre does not advance in our estimation, nor does the drama become in any way more intense or vital because of Melville's assertions of a highly respectable past. The technique is unrecognisable in its clumsiness. Melville begins circumspectly enough: "Pierre was the only son of an affluent, and haughty widow" (Bk. I, Chap. ii). Soon we are told that "the Glendinning deeds by which their estate had so long been held, bore the ciphers of three Indian kings. . ." Very early it is apparent that the subtlety of Moby Dick will be absent; instead of the noted accretive process, Melville breaks cover to challenge polemically the bases of English aristocracy and to defend American genealogies:

> The monarchical world very generally imagines, that in demagogical America the sacred Past hath no fixed statues erected in it, but all things irreverently

seethe and boil in the vulgar caldron of an everlasting uncrystalizing Present. . . . In this matter we will--not superciliously, but in fair spirit--compare pedigrees England, and strange as it may seem at the first blush, not without some claim to equality (Bk. I, Chap. iii).

Melville goes on, with little skill, to write in some detail of the illegitimacies in the English aristocratic line, referring to the "bye-blows of kings," and those "whose ancestress could n o t well avoid being a mother, it is true, but had accidentally omitted the preliminary rite." Melville advances instead an American aristocracy, "the Randolphs for example, one of whose ancestors, in King James' time, married Pocahontas, the Indian princess, and in whose blood therefore an underived aboriginal royalty was flowing over two hundred years ago."

All this is supposed to aid the story of Pierre, who describes himself to his mother as "First Lady in waiting to the Dowager Duchess Glendinning" (Bk. 1, Chap. V). In that household "a bountiful appetite, was not only no vulgar reproach, but a right royal grace and honor to Pierre" (Bk. 1, Chap. vi). Describing Lucy Tartan, Melville muses that "a beautiful woman is born Queen of men and women both, as Mary Stuart was born Queen of Scots, whether men or women" (Bk. II, Chap. ii). And later: "But whither indeed should Lucy Tartan conduct us, but among mighty Queens, and all other creatures of high degree" (Bk. II, Chap. ii). But Melville has nowhere to go with this. It matters little to anyone that an American ancestry can be aristocratic or that the English royal line is "impure"; that which was absolutely needed in Moby Dick is a liability in Pierre, and Melville has to resort to crash programs to broaden the character of Pierre and provide material for the unfolding tale; in Chapter XVI, with the book two-thirds complete, Melville tells us for the first time that Pierre is a writer and that a major work is being written. The novel gains a reprieve of sorts, as we observe Melville painting his portrait of the artist as a young man. Pierre, by this time, had already failed.

Melville would not repeat this error in Israel Potter. Within the limitations of an admittedly less ambitious work, Melville achieves a greater control of symbolic devices, so subtle as at times to be almost imperceptible, than he had ever experienced before, even in Moby Dick. As for the royal metaphor, neither three eminences of American history nor one real king tempt him into the same traps. As Israel labors in the brickyard at the dreary job of ladling, he speaks his mind: "Kings as clowns are codgers--who ain't a nobody?" (Chap. XXIII). And yet Melville is aware of the advantages of kingship and elevation in literature and even more aware that he faced special problems in attempting to render dramatically the life and sufferings of so economically, socially and culturally deprived a person as Israel Potter:

> The gloomiest and truthfulest dramatist seldom chooses for his theme the calamities, however extraordinary, of inferior and private persons; least of all, the pauper's; admonished by the fact, that to the craped palace of the king lying in state, thousands of starers shall throng; but few feel enticed to the shanty, where, like a pealed knucklebone, grins the unupholstered corpse of the beggar (Chap. XXV).

In Israel Potter Melville finally faced the artistic implications of his "ruthless democracy"; it was a challenge that entailed little less than an overhauling of his art.

Chapter Two

Old Tombstone Retouched

If Israel Potter does not presently enjoy the highest regard of Melville critics, the work was more eagerly welcomed by readers and reviewers when it was first published in serial form in Putnam's Monthly Magazine starting from July of 1854, and in its completed shape in March of the following year. After the second installment had appeared, the Morning Courier and New York Enquirer noted that it made pleasant reading and showed an improved Melville, particularly in its style, which was "manly, direct and clear."[1] After almost every monthly issue of Putnam's, the newspaper generally noted the publication and never retracted its original praise for what it felt was Melville's lighter tone and more intelligible style. In March of 1855 the Boston Post Review added its voice in the same key, calling the story, which had just been published in its final form, "a book, not great, not remarkable for any particular in it, but of a curt, manly, independent tone, dealing with truth honestly, and telling it feelingly."[2] Two months later, the National Magazine reviewed the work as "a story of the revolutionary times, written in a half-comic, half patriotic being, yet withal exceedingly attractive, and not a little instructive"; and it was able to add some dimension to the critical viewpoint with an observation that "a tinge of obscure sarcasm pervades the book,

16

most apparent in its dedication to the Bunker Hill Monument."[3]

The Revue des Deux Mondes provided a more searching commentary on the work in July, 1855:

> Ce livre semble en effet une tentative pour déployer dans le cadre d'un récit populaire deux qualités essentielles de l'esprit américaine l'amour-propre démocratique et l'orgeuil national. ... One retrouve l'amour du heros pousse en quelque sorte jusqu'à la susceptibilité, la narration lente et detaillée, la calque fidele et minutieux de la réalité, l'apotheose et la sublimisation, ... Il le presente comme le type de ces vertus sue la terre ennemie, comme le symbole de la démocratie dans un pays aristocratique.[4]

In general, the reception of the book on both sides of the Atlantic was mildy favorable, with certain qualifications noted by the most comprehensive harvester of Melville's reviews: in America, "the lack of studies of any length, the diminution of the total number of reviews and notices in the case of Israel Potter, ... boded no good for its author's ultimate reputation."[5] In Britain, reviewers appeared to be less enthusiastic about a work apparently so anti-British. But after reading the first half the reviewer of the London Leader "felt disposed to rank Israel Potter as incomparably the best work that Mr. Melville had yet written."[6] The Athenaeum was less kind, and Melville could not have been pleased with its crumb of approbation that "his book, with all its faults, is not a bad shilling's worth for any railway station reader, who does not object to small type and a style the glories of which are nebulous."[7]

The most significant aspect of the book's critical reputation in this century is the extent to which it has been ignored. The massive revaluation of the life and work of Melville that transformed his name from obscurity to its present honored position passed by Israel Potter with little more than muttered apologies for an apparently indefensible work. Until the sixties, an attempt to gather material written in appreciation of Israel Potter would have been a perfunctory exercise, a gathering, with only a few exceptions, of critical crumbs. For example, Melville "quarrels with God" for hundreds of pages in Laurance Thompson's work without once bringing up Israel's name, and Milton Stern minutely examines the "fine-hammered steel of Herman Melville" without finding a trace of the refugee. The dismissal of the book has become standard in the necessarily selective surveys; Darrel Abel writes: "Israel Potter is not full of secondary or deep meanings . . . . It is a circumstantial tale of adventure, . . . a succession of episodes rather than a plotted narrative. Its interest is more thematic than dramatic."[8] For Marcus Cunliffe, the road after Pierre is downhill, and Israel Potter is a "painfully desolate historical novel."[9] A recent study on pacifism and rebellion in Melville's writing talks of "an enjoyable but trivial historical novel."[10] In earlier studies, Matthiessen concluded that the book was a "failure," indicative of Melville's exhausted vitality;[11] Newton Arvin finds impression of "great and unemcumbered power," but summarizes that the book is "hardly more than a heap of sketches, some of them brilliant, for a masterpiece that never got composed. The use of another man's book, in this case as in 'Benito Cereno', was a literary deadfall for Melville."[12]

There are contrary views, however few in number or unconvincing in evidence. Richard Chase's Herman Melville applauded the "light-hearted and unpretentious book," reminiscent of Melville's earlier novels, but more beguiling than most of those. There are somber depths in the book, but these are less oppressive than in Typee. The self-conscious erudition, the slightly oafish philosophizing of Omoo and Mardi Melville has pretty much purged by the time he arrives at Israel Potter. His style had become more mature, lighter, more sunny and open."[13] Less convincing is Yvor Winters' undocumented assertion that "Israel Potter, the life of an American patriot of the Revolutionary War, is one of the few great novels of pure adventure in English; it comes after Moby Dick in point of time, and probably surpasses all the works preceding Moby Dick save, possibly, Mardi."[14] More accurate possibly is the opinion of Professor Rosenberry that Israel Potter is "a fair candidate for the Most Underrated American Novel."[15]

Sifting through all the condemnations and qualifications, the faint praise and loud damnings, it is possible to isolate the general critical impressions of Israel Potter, looking not so much for consensus as for some common areas of considered opinion. The early praise of lucidity of style has survived; few seem to find much that is presistently opaque in the novel. Linked with this, as if clarity were a literary sin for Melville, is the impression of the work's shallowness, expressed simultaneously with praise for any or all of the three characterisations of Benjamin Franklin, John Paul Jones and Ethan Allen. This shallowness is seen as deriving from three principal factors: the timidity of Melville after the scorn heaped on Pierre and the ignoring of Moby Dick, Melville's overdependence on the Life and Remarkable Adventures of Israel R. Potter, and the demands of the magazine readership for material that was necessarily episodic and preferably diverting. Connected with all these three, and, in the final analysis, most damaging of all, there is the notion that Israel Potter is an extraneous part of the Melville Library, one in which he was only barely involved, dictated by a story already written by the old soldier, motivated either by a "miserable compulsion," or by the need for money. This is also the least defensible of critical opinions.

Melville encouraged talk of shallowness, albeit unwittingly, when he sent the first sixty pages of manuscript to George Putnam; after discussing financial and editorial matters concerning the serial form, Melville saw fit to assure Putnam that the new book was no Pierre in the making: "I engage that the story shall contain nothing of any sort to shock the fastidious. There will be very little reflective writing it it; nothing weighty; it is adventure. As for its interest, I shall try to sustain that as well as I can."[16] It is interesting that Melville saw a difference between the aspect of adventure and the "interest" of the work. One should remember, though, that Melville almost invariably set out to write books that would please, that he never consciously set out to "shock the fastidious." Consider the revealing letter to Richard Bentley concerning Melville's new work, Pierre, and one sees that Melville, like so many authors, knew not what he had done. Rejecting Bentley's editorial conditions, Melville affirms that "more especially am I impelled to decline those overtures upon the ground that my new book possessing unquestionable novelty, as regards my former ones,--treating of utterly new scenes & characters;--and, as I believe, very much more calculated for popularity than anything you have yet published of mine."[17] In any event, Melville had written to Putnam concerning plans for Israel Potter most likely before the work was finished or even half-completed; the latter to Bentley had been sent at a similar stage in the development of Pierre.

And Melville was by nature deprecatory about his work, "botches" as he referred to them in writing to Hawthorne, "spoiled by the necessity of trying to compromise between what he was most moved to write and what the public would buy."[18] Melville's initial criticism of Israel Potter was premature. It is even questionable that he knew precisely where he was going and with what intensity, when he delivered those first pages to George Putnam.

It is obvious that when those first sixty pages of manuscript were being written, Melville's "tattered copy" of Israel's original work, "rescued by the merest chance from the rag-pickers"[19] was close at hand on Melville's writing desk. The Melville scholar goes to the Life and Remarkable Adventures in the same way as the Shakespearean interested in Othello goes to Cinthio's novella, and with the same pertinent questions. How much did our author borrow? How much did he modify? And what did he positively eschew as he applied his personal creativity and discrimination to the task of fashioning a work authentically his? Melville's word is not enough; it is deliberately misleading. From Israel's little book, he writes,

> the present account has been drawn, which with the exception of some expansions, and additions of historic and personal details, and one or two shiftings of scene, may, perhaps, be not unfitly regarded something in the light of a delapidated old tombstone retouched.[20]

The tone of the entire dedication is light and bantering, as befits a speech addressed to a monument, though it is salted with irony at the futility of the heroism commended by the monument, which is "the national commemorator of such of the anonymous privates of July 17, 1775, who may never have received other requital than the solid reward of your granite."[21]

It is therefore necessary to look for ourselves for the dependence of Melville on Potter's work. That work itself appears to be seriously over-rated as a piece of art. Critical suggestion that Melville should have found in the Life and Remarkable Adventures "ideal material for a profound and moving work,"[22] is as misleading as the frequently asserted opinion that Melville's text and Potter's are in a major way semblative:

> Compare Herman Melville's fine tale of
> Israel Potter with the humble account
> which it rewrites, and notice how close-
> ly the artist follows the veteran's story
> line. Melville recognised an honest,
> dramatic, and peculiarly American re-
> cord in the odd little book hawked
> through the country by Yankee pedlers.[23]

This agrees with Melville's own assertion in the dedication that his novel "preserves, almost as a reprint, Israel Potter's autobiographical story." In fact, little in that dedication can be taken at its face value, and while Melville does follow the old man's tale, he does so for only six of twenty six chapters; even within these six, the most ultimately significant occurrences are additions of Melville, and the book itself achieves no stature until Melville shakes off the restrictive hold of the <u>Life and Remarkable Adventures</u>.

For Potter's little book was neither particularly honest nor significantly dramatic; it is peculiarly American only as far as it serves the propagandistic aims of the author and his publisher. All we know is that one Israel Potter left America and was some fifty years a-coming home. He had left his home as a British subject before the Declaration of Independence, had spent almost all of the intervening years in Britain, had never gone to the American consulate even when relations between the two nations had fallen into peace; he had married an English lass and fathered English children. It is difficult to see how the court that tried his case could have arrived at any other decision concerning his right to a pension, unless out of an extra-legal sympathy; it is a little unfair to those dead jurors to say that "America was far too busy in the conquest of itself to give death [Israel's coming death] anything more than the platitudinous comfort of words."[24]

Perhaps old Potter really expected that he deserved a pension for the brief acts of service to his country; in any event, his need on arrival back in America was for money, and if the courts would not provide it, he hoped that the little volume would. Melville, who could have read this work no other way than critically, the way in which he must have read all pieces of literature, noted in the dedication that Israel must have employed a ghost to pen the tale, "written, probably, not by himself, but taken down from his lips by another." Whether the ghost suggested the writing of the tale to Israel or Israel approached the printer with his story is unclear; what is abundantly obvious is that they knew what they were after: "it is to obtain if possible a humble pittance as a remuneration, in part, for the unprecedented privations and sufferings of which he has been the unfortunate subject, that he is now induced to present the public with the following concise and simple narration of the most extraordinary incidents of his life" (Life, p. 4).

The prospect of good sales wonderfully refreshed Potter's memory after fifty years. He remembers the day of his departure quite clearly, that it was a Sunday, what time he left the house, the precise ruse employed in quitting the premises, that it was a "warm summer's night," that he later agreed "to labour for one month for the sum of six dollars." Names of people and places provide no trouble, distances are clear: for example, after a fire at sea, he remembers distinctly the smallest details:

> Orders were immediately thereupon given by the captain to hoist out the long boat, which was found in such a leaky condition as to require constant bailing to keep her afloat; we had only time to put on board a small quantity of bread, a firkin of butter and a ten-gallon keg of water, when we embarked, eight in number, to trust ourselves to the mercy of the waves. . . (Life, p. 11).

This is suggestive of a compromised honesty; the whole work challenges our credulity; he sets sail "about the 8th of December", after being captured he engages in a plot with his fellow prisoners, "72 in number" (Life, p. 19).

The attempt here is not simply to cast doubt on Potter's accuracy but rather to stress that the work is not the simple, ingenuous tale of an old man who had suffered long and whose life provided interesting parallels with that of a distinguished American in search of a new work. It is a story in which artifice is attempted, if not art, and as such it presented particular problems, as well as suggestions, to Melville as he sought to convert it to his own use. In his own maladroit way, Potter's ghost-writer was working hard at transforming, through manipulation of fact, the life story of Israel Potter from that of an aimless drifter, too incompetent or too unenthused to take the few positive steps needed to go back to his homeland, into a saga of affliction in which Israel would loom as a kind of tragic hero.

But not even in the loosest sense is Potter a tragic hero, or the <u>Life and Remarkable Adventures</u> a real tragedy; it is a book <u>about</u> tragic circumstances. For fifty pages we have adventure, as Israel leaves home, is captured, eludes his captors, fights and flees to live other days. But once this is over the book settles down for another fifty pages almost totally devoid of plot or character development. Half of the book is nothing more than a catalogue of urban horrors, wild-eyed stories of crime in the streets and sustained deprivation in the ghetto neighborhoods, with the propagandistic insistence all along that this is a fair sampling of English life, and that America treats its own children far better. It is an overt appeal to patriotism and pride, but it has very little to do with Potter. After relating an incident when he was robbed of a few pennies by a gang of bullies ("the reader has undoubtedly heard that the city of London and its suburbs, is always more or less infested with gangs of nefarious wretches, who come under the denomination of Robbers, Pickpockets, Shoplifters, Swindlers, Beggars, &c."), Potter proceeds to enumerate instances of the cruelty of the London environment:

> A Mr. Wylde while passing through Marlbourough Street, in a chaise, was stopped by a footpad, who, on demanding his money, received a few shillings, but being dissatisfied with the little booty he obtained, still kept a pistol at Mr. Wylde's head, and on the latter's attempting gently to turn it aside, the villain fired, and lodged seven slugs in his head and breast, which caused instant death--Mr. W. expired in the arms of his son and grandson without a groan (<u>Life</u>, p. 65).

And then there was Mr. Greenhill, seized by three footpads, who "after robbing him of his notes, watch and hat gave him two severe cuts on his head and left him in that deplorable state in

the road"(ibid.).
From all this Israel concludes:

> Thus have I endeavoured to furnish the reader with the particulars of a few of the vices peculiar to a large portion of the inhabitants of the city of London--to these might be added a thousand other misdemeanours of a less criminal nature, daily practised by striplings from the age of six, to the hoary headed of ninety!--this I assure my readers is a picture correctly delineated and not too highly wrought of a city famous for its magnificence, and where I was doomed to spend more than forty years of my life, and in which time pen, ink, and paper would fail, were I to attempt to record the various instances of misery and want that attended me and my poor devoted family (Life, p. 66).

Where Israel surely failed before the law courts, and where he fails in the Life and Remarkable Adventures, is in convincing us that he was indeed doomed to spend such a long time away. The question that constantly recurs asks simply for an explanation for Israel's prolonged stay. If London and England provided such hardships, and if he had remained in spirit the American patriot he professed to be in applying for a pension, what took him so long in his voyage home? The court was unconvinced and the reader is unconvinced; the author of the Life and Remarkable Adventures demonstrates an overwhelming desire to convince, but has so poor a case that he succeeds only in making Potter a slinking, evasive and spineless figure; by the end of the book we seriously doubt the central role he gives himself in so many incidents, as we doubt that any man could remember the minute details apparently so clear in his mind after fifty or sixty years.

It is important to stress that the primary aim in examining the little novel is not to decide whether it could be successful in what it set out to do, but rather to ascertain how the novel, and especially the character of its principal figure, must have appeared to a reader of the high literary sophistication of Herman Melville. The mass readership of a scandal or confessional magazine become fairly involved with the lives of the characters; to the educated reader the same material is sheer transparency and triteness. What attracted Melville to the character of Israel Potter was not the latter's heroic tragedy, as is so often assumed in criticism, but the refugee's erraticism, his evasion of responsibility, his lack of high ideals, his constant recourse to subterfuge to protect his interests: in short, Melville saw Israel as Everyman. In Life and Remarkable Adventures, he remains an ordinary man. Melville nourished his character through experience into a higher degree of worthiness. The real Israel Potter never learnt much from his life; he left home a foolish, impetuous boy; he returned over half a century later a foolish, querulous old man.

The very aspects which made Life and Remarkable Adventures sell fairly briskly during its brief day precluded any possibility of Israel assuming tragic literary proportion: the ghost writer overstates the case for Israel's escapades, and overloads the chamber of horrors in which he was supposed to have spent his life. Everyone constantly denies Israel his due or tries to cheat him. He leaves home because his sweetheart's parents are adamant that he should not have their daughter: "I was reprimanded and threatened with more severe punishment, if my visits were not discontinued"(p. 5). His second job after leaving home finds him assisting a traveller with boating chores, and again he is abused: "It was with some difficulty and not until I had procured a writ. . . that I obtained from my last employer the four dollars which he had agreed to pay me for my services" (p. 7). His next employment finds him working 200 acres of new land for four months, in return for the promise of a deed to the acreage. Here again, the owner refuses to keep that promise and Israel moves on, once again cheated. He does well as a trapper and planter, returns home with a handsome amount of money, gives most of it to his parents, promises to stay at home and hopes for a change of their attitude to his love-affair,

> but, in this, I soon found that I was mistaken; for, although overjoyed to see me alive, whom they had supposed dead, no sooner did they find that my long absence had rather increased than diminished my attachment for their neigh-

> bour's daughter, than their resentment
> and opposition appeared to increase in
> proportion. . . (Life, p. 10).

and Israel must take to the road again. He takes passage on a ship; it catches fire. He goes whaling, does fairly well, but gives it up eventually, "perfectly sick of the sea"(p. 12).

Israel takes part in the Battle of Bunker Hill, and this must have been the central point of his case for a pension, his principal role in the service of the foetal republic, and he does not let us forget that he was there:

> the conflict, which was a sharp and
> severe one, is still fresh in my memory,
> and cannot be forgotten by me while the
> scars of the wounds which I then receiv-
> ed, remain to remind me of it! (Life, p. 16).

The old soldier, perhaps with advantage, remembers the deeds he did on his St. Crispin's day:

> A blow with a cutlass was aimed at my
> head by a British officer, which I par-
> ried and received only a slight cut with
> the point of my right arm near the elbow,
> which I was then unconscious of, but
> this slight wound cost my antagonist at
> the moment a much more serious one,
> which effectually dis-armed him, for
> with one well directed stroke I depriv-
> ed him of the power of very soon again
> measuring swords with a "yankee rebel!"
> (ibid.).

Israel the hero goes to sea, helping in the blockade of Boston with several other soldiers. Their ship is captured. Compare two accounts, one of them Potter's, about the latter's initiative and place in a plot to take command of the British vessel. John Vial, in a deposition on behalf of Potter in Rhode Island in 1823, writes:

> I do remember an affair which took
> place during our voyage to England

> which caused Potter to suffer a great deal more than perhaps he otherwise would--a number of the crew of the Washington formed a plan to rise and take the frigate but was defeated in their purpose, among which I believe Potter was one...(<u>Life</u>, p. 107).

Israel remembers his role perfectly; there is no question in his mind who engineered the complot:

> When two or three days out I projected a scheme (with the assistance of my fellow prisoners, 72 in number) to take the ship, in which we should undoubtedly have succeeded, as we had a number of stout fellows on board, had it not been for the treachery of a renegade Englishman, who betrayed us--as I was pointed out by this fellow as the principal in the plot . . . (<u>Life</u>, p. 14).

And once again, long-suffering Israel R. Potter suffers for his country.

Taken by his captors to England, Israel demonstrates the kind of basic common-sense that some would call "Yankee ingenuity" and find the basis of the "Americanness" of the book. He is allowed a moment's freedom to facilitate bodily processes and immediately takes to his heels, running "about four miles without once halting." He walks until he is ten miles from his original place; then, after a chase "of nearly a mile," he is recaptured. He is made to dance a jig by one of his keepers "who observed that he had frequently heard it mentioned that the yankees were extraordinary dancers" (possessing, one supposes, natural rhythm), and entertains the company with his dancing as they drank themselves into intoxication:

> with the full determination, however that if John Bull was to be thus diverted at the expense of an unfortunate prisoner of war, Uncle Jonathan should come in for his part of the sport before morn-

28   Melville's ISRAEL POTTER

> ing, by showing them a few Yankee steps which they then little dreamed of (Life, p. 23).

He escapes, and once again we are treated to an account of Israel's extraordinary physical abilities, which Melville will carefully modify, in the interests of general credibility, when he writes the tale:

> In groping about I met with a fruit tree situated with within ten or twelve feet of the wall, which I ascended as expeditiously as possible, and by an extraordinary leap from the branches reached the top of the wall, and was in an instant on the opposite side (Life, p. 25).

Here is Melville's account:

> But a fruit-tree grew close to the wall. Springing into it desperately, handcuffed as he was, Israel leaps atop of the barrier, and without pausing to see where he is, drops himself to the ground on the other side, and once more lets grow all his wings (Ch. III).

The first period of normalcy in his English sojourn comes with his employment by Sir John Millet, but before this he is subjected by circumstances to "four days of intolerable hunger" and deepening despair, until he learns patience and reaches "a baker's shop in the neighbourhood, where with my four last remaining pennies, . . . I purchased two two-penny loaves." Israel has a passion for small economic details.

After recuperating and earning a livelihood at Sir John's, Potter is summoned by a Squire Woodcock, an English gentleman sympathetic to the newly declared independent republic of the United States; there, he tells us, he is introduced to Horne Tooke and James Bridges, taking care to note that his publication and disclousure can no longer harm them:

> As all three of these gentlemen have long since paid the debt of nature, and are placed beyond the reach of such as might be disposed to persecute or reproach them for their disloyalty, I can now with perfect safety disclose their names--names which ought to be dear to every true American (Life, p. 47).

He is sent as a courier to Paris and meets Benjamin Franklin, who, he claims, "for nearly an hour. . . conversed with me in the most agreeable and instructive manner, and listened to the tale of my sufferings with much apparent interest." The author of the Life and Remarkable Adventures does not waste any opportunity to summon witnesses from the grave to Potter's defense in his claim for a pension:

> I am confident . . . that had it been a possible thing for that great and good man (whose humanity and generosity have been the theme of infinitely abler pens than mine) to have lived to this day, I should not have petitioned my country in vain for a momentary enjoyment of that provision, which has been extended to so great a portion of my fellow soldiers; and whose hardships and deprivations, in the cause of their country, could not I am sure have been half so great as mine (Life, p. 51).

This meeting with Dr. Franklin, whatever its degree of cordiality, was the last service rendered by Israel to his country; his little book is only half-completed, and the next fifty pages recall his life in London in the various occupations of brick builder, to which he barely alludes, gardener and chair-mender. His hopes of returning to America are thwarted when communication between London and Paris is severely curtailed; the war was lingering on and peace was nowhere in sight, when Potter gave himself new responsibility and effectively divided his loyalty.

> I became more reconciled to my situation, and contracted an intimacy with

> a young woman whose parents were poor but respectable, and who I soon after married (Life, p. 58).

But Potter could not complete his story without at some point facing directly the issue of his culpability in not returning home before extreme old age. It is not a very convincing statement, but with the Peace Treaty signed between the United States and Britain, a statement was obviously necessary:

> An opportunity indeed now presented for me to return once more to my native country, after so long an absence, had I possessed the means; but such was the high price demanded for a passage, and such had been my low wages, and the expenses attending the support of even a small family in London, that I found myself at this time in possession of funds hardly sufficient to defray the expense of my own passage, and much less that of my wife and child --hence the only choice left me was either to desert them, and thereby subject them (far separated from me) to the frowns of an uncharitable people, or to content myself to remain with them and partake of a portion of that wretchedness which even my presence could not avert. When the affairs of the American Government had become so far regulated as to support a Consul at the British court, I might indeed have availed myself individually, of the opportunity which presented of procuring a passage home at the Government's expence; but as this was a privilege that could not be extended to my wife and child, my regard for them prevented my embracing the only means provided by my country for the return of her captured soldiers and seamen (Life, p. 57).

As if to counterbalance any impression that he might have been negligent in not showing greater initiative in getting home, Potter steps up his assault on the reader's sense of pity, there is a noticeable coloring of language, an element of desperation as the Life and Remarkable Adventures enters its last stages. Potter, unable to pay his creditors, is visited by a bailiff, " who seizing me with the claws of a tiger, dragged me from my poor afflicted family and inhumanly thrust me into prison!" He tries to reason with the man responsible for sending the bailiff, but "he proved to be one of those human beasts, who, having no soul, take pleasure in tormenting that of others," and Potter assures the readers that "London contains not an inconsiderable number."

Potter's increasingly intense description of his personal vale of tears, while it is so often too shrill in tone and too generally unrelieved, does not leave us always unaffected. Enough is known of England's inhuman application of capital punishment in the eighteenth century to support his story of the one Bellamy, executed for a crime "which distresses in his family, almost unexampled, had in a moment of despair, compelled him to commit." There is, too, the revoltingly effective account of the poor widow, destitute and with five small children, feeding them at last with a roasted dog. Potter's personal misfortune, once he settles down to life in England, also rings true. He describes his daily routine as a mender of chairs, an occupation unpredictable in its remuneration and generally humiliating in its practice. He explains that with the end of the war the market is flooded with cheap labor and that desperation is the common lot of the impoverished workers. His eulogy for his wife, who dies under the hardships of the family's deprived condition, is simple and moving:

> I felt very sensibly the irreparable loss of one who had been my companion in adversity, as well as in prosperity; and when blessed with health, had afforded me by her industry that assistance, without which, the sufferings of our poor children would have been greater if possible than what they were (Life, p. 89).

He is not up to this standard when he spends a whole page telling of a rainy Saturday when, after failing to find employment and reward, he stands staring at the meat on a butcher's stand until the proprietor tossed him a beef's heart in a gesture that moves Potter's son to tears of joy. Or when he feels it really necessary to tell us that after walking the two miles to the American consul's office, he was "so much exhausted as to be obligated to ascend the steps on my hands and knees."

  The American consul arranges with much personal generosity for the return of Potter to the United States, but the latter soon discovers that there are more misfortunes awaiting him. Sailing over on the ship, he is uncivilly treated by the sailors, all of whom, he quickly points out, were not Americans. Worse is to come. His brothers, not surprisingly, had presumed him dead, had divided the estate and had resettled in parts unknown of the United States; Israel is completely without home. As a last resort he petitions Congress for a pension, "and I would to God that I could add, for the honour of my country, that the application met with its deserving success. . . yet, on no other principle, than that I was absent from the country when the pension law was passed--my Petition was REJECTED ! ! !"(sic). His approach at the end is direct, though his argument is difficult to accept:

> Reader, I have been for 30 years...
> subject, in a foreign country, to almost
> all the miseries with which poor human
> nature is capable of being inflicted...
> It is my sincere prayer that this strange
> and unprecedented circumstance, of
> witholding from me that reward which
> they have so generally bestowed on
> others, may never be told in Europe
> or published in the streets of London,
> least it reach the ears of some who had
> the effrontery to declare to me personally, that for the active part that I had
> taken in the "rebellious war" misery
> and starvation would ultimately be my
> reward! (Life, pp. 105-106).

This was the material with which Melville elected to work; as for the man Potter, there is abundant other evidence within the Life and Remarkable Adventures to indicate that if his suffering was inhuman, and this is not quite clear even after one reads all the horrors related in his book, that he himself was very much of flesh and bone.

Unlike Melville's Ethan Allen, Potter had preferred deception and disguise to the defiant stand. When he is first captured by the British and joins the plot to take over the ship, he never admits to the patriotic act but rather protests his innocence until his accuser is discredited. His various escapes show deviousness rather than noble defiance; he resorts to disguise so often (Melville will use this with great subtlety) that at one point he pauses both to congratulate himself and, as if aware that he was cutting a dubious figure, generally apologise:

> The reader will perceive that I had now become almost an adept at deception, which I would not however have so frequently practiced, had not self-preservation demanded it (Life, p. 30).

Though apprehensive at meeting Sir John Millet because of the reputation of the "tyrannical and domineering disposition of the rich and purse-proud of England," he soon settles in very nicely with the aristocrat; Melville will toughen his resistance to nobility. After working in the royal gardens for some time, he is addressed briefly by the King himself. As in his meeting with Benjamin Franklin, Potter is soon overwhelmed:

> The familar manner in which I had been interrogated by his Majesty, had I must confess a tendency in some degree to prepossesses me in his favour--I atleast suspected him to possess a disposition less tyrannical, and capable of better view than what had been imputed to him; and as I had frequently heard it represented in America, that uninfluenced by such of his ministers, as unwisely disregarded the reiterated complaints of the American people, he would have been foremost to have redressed their grievances, of which they so justly complained (Life, p. 44).

Melville will point out that Israel, while having much of the gentleness of the dove, "is not wholly without the wisdom of the Serpent " (Ch. III).

When Melville suggested that his own novel Israel Potter might, "perhaps, be not unfitly regarded something in the light of a delapidated old tombstone retouched," the safest conclusion we can infer is that he had found the Life and Remarkable Adventures having precisely the vivacity of a tombstone; what he was after in writing a novel was, of course, life, and there remained to Melville the self-imposed task of revitalising the dead material of Israel Potter's work. For whatever attraction initially brought Melville to examine the life of Potter must have had its supplementary elements of repulsion because of the detailed picture of the man and his philosophy of life painted allegedly with his own hand in the Life and Remarkable Adventures. Melville's changes to the original story reveal more than artistic criticism of Potter's plain tale, though that artistic criticism must be documented in any examination; those changes reveal Melville's reflection of the personality and responses of Potter to the tribulations that beset him from the time he left his father's home to the moment of his death after those fifty years of exile. However profound his instinctive sympathy for the unfortunate refugee, Melville did not accept without intense qualification Potter's reactions and opinions; if Melville identified his own misfortunes with those of the old soldier, as critics are wont too easily to assume, it was an identification that did not exclude criticism, eschewment and adaptation. The portrait of Potter which we have observed emerging from a reading of the autobiography is not altogether a salubrious one; if Melville accepted the lure of the superficial similarity between his life-experience and that of Potter, there are also significant departures that tell us a great deal about Melville.

There is no denying, however, that after the first chapter of Israel Potter, which is most profitably discussed only when the entire symbolic framework of the novel is under review, Melville turns to Israel's own pages and adheres for five further chapters (Chs. 2-6) with remarkable tenacity. This is not to say that Melville does not seriously embellish as he goes along; he cleverly modifies the character of Israel, carefully converts him into a more believable personage, and sows the early symbolic seeds so conspicuously absent in Life and Remarkable Adventures.

But in those five chapters after his opening invention Melville stayed with the story to an extent that surprises; he appeared to be reasonably satisfied with the style and content of Potter's literary sense. Melville changes the first person narrative to the third person, and relaxes the terse depositional tone with which Potter initially imbues his narrative. Potter starts with no philosophising, no general remarks: "I was born of reputable parents in the town of Cranston, State of Rhode Island, August 1, 1744. --I continued with my parents there in the full enjoyment of parental affection and indulgence, until I arrived at the age of eighteen. . . ." Melville does not altogether despise this crispness; compare, for example, his adherence to the letter of Potter's writing. This is the <u>Life and Remarkable Adventures</u> relating Israel's initial flight from home:[25]

> It was on Sunday, while the family were at meeting, that I packed up as many articles of my clothing as could be contained in a pocket handkerchief, which, with a small quantity of provisions, I conveyed to and secreted in a piece of woods in the rear of my father's house until about 9 in the evening, when with the pretence of retiring to bed, I pass- into a back room and from thence out of a back door and hastened to the spot where I had deposited my clothes, &c (<u>Life</u>, p. 6).

When Melville came to tell the story, he shows a textual fidelity that left little to his own imagination:

> It was on Sunday, while the family were gone to a farmhouse church near by, that he packed up as much of his clothing as might be contained in a handkerchief, which, with a small quantity of provision, he hid in a piece of woods in the rear of the house. He then returned, and continued in the house till about nine in the evening, when, pretending to go to bed, he passed out of a back door, and hastened to the woods for his bundle (Ch. 2).

36   Melville's ISRAEL POTTER

Melville removes some cobwebs from Potter's style here and there, adding a bit of polish to the narrative, but obviously feels comfortable in the presence of the original source. Yet his changes are very important. They demonstrate that Melville, quite early in his novel and even as he almost transcribes portions of Potter's book, is looking ahead.

Potter did not mention the month of his departure. Melville informs us that "it was a sultry night in July," placing this initial action in the great American revolutionary month. It is the same type of calendar conspiracy, by no means a major artistic stroke, that he employs so beguilingly in having the Confidence-Man start on April 1, All Fools' Day, and published on the same day in 1857. In Israel Potter, where Melville will raise important questions about the possible subversion of the ideals of the American revolution and the American character, July is never far away. Israel leaves home in July, watches Washington take command of the troops "on the third of July"; he will eventually have his great hallucination concerning life at home on the slopes of the Housatonic on "one fair half-day in the July of 1800" (Ch. XXV), and returns to the United States after his decades of exile on the fourth day of July, when he narrowly escapes "being run over by a patriotic triumphal car in the procession" (Ch. XXVI). For good measure, the first installment of the story appeared in Putnam's Monthly Magazine early in July of 1854, subtitled "A Fourth of July Story." Thoreau, of course, also set out on his revolutionary experiment at Walden on the Fourth of July.

But Melville's main problem lay with the humanisation of his young Potter; the original refugee represented in the Life and Remarkable Adventures lacked soul, relating his departure from home without the slightest trace of real emotion, indeed, without any recorded qualm. He had merely "formed the determination to leave them, for the purpose of seeking another home and other friends." Melville becomes entangled in the memories of his own "Redburn complex," and sends Israel away from the hearth a picture of lachrymose innocence united to manly determination:

>Like the leaflets of that evergreen, all the fibres of his heart trembled within him; tears fell from his eyes. But he thought of the tyranny of his father, and what seemed to him the faithless-

> ness of his love; and shouldering his
> bundle, arose, and marched on (Ch.
> II).

Israel thus becomes an apparently more sensitive young man in the hands of Melville; the vicarious autobiographical overtones are naturally pleasant. Melville, for all the restraint he employs in staying close to the Potter text, cannot resist a slight eddy of philosophical lyricism as the young man decides to ship out:

> A hermitage in the forest is the refuge
> of the narrow-minded misanthrope; a
> hammock on the ocean is the asylum for
> the generous distressed. The ocean
> brims with natural griefs and tragedies;
> and into that watery immensity of ter-
> ror, man's private grief is lost like a
> drop (Ch. 2).

If Potter too obviously thrust himself at the center of the incidents (for example, the ship-board plot or his part in the Franklin-Horne Tooke conspiracy), Melville has no obligation to refrain from building Israel's heroic stature, since he is not supposed to be **telling** the truth. Thus we find that Melville gives Potter a boost when his ship catches fire on his initial trip away from home. Israel catches at a fragment of the flyingjib, "tanned with smoke and its edge blackened with fire," and t h i s proves to be the saviour of the crew after they abandon s h ip. Melville is also stirring other memories when he deals with the real Potter's two whaling voyages. All Potter remarked in his book about these two trips was that the first had been "short and successful," and that on the other (with characteristic self-pity) he had "experienced almost all the hardships and deprivations peculiar to Whalemen in long voyages." Melville tells us instead that "he hunted the leviathan . . . for sixteen months; returning at length with a brimming hold"; he goes to the South Seas a nd "there, promoted to be harpooner, Israel . . . now further intensified his aim, by darting the whale-lance."

Melville is more exclusive in other aspects and suggestions of the Potter tale; he does not mention Potter's duplicity in recounting the tale of the ship-board plot, when Potter after telling the reader that the idea had been formulated by himself denied having anything to do with it. In Melville's story Potter merely holds his tongue until his accuser is discredited. As for his exaggerations, Melville indicates the skeptical response to Potter's claim that he had run four miles in his first escape: "He runs four miles (so he afterwards affirmed) without halting" (Ch. III). The real Potter told of meeting a ditch "upward of 19 feet in breadth, and of what depth I could not determine" (Life, p. 31), which he leapt across with the greatest of ease. This is too much for Melville; he leaves the depth "undiscoverable," but reduces the width to a more manageable ten feet.

Potter's ambivalent patriotism, caused no doubt by his long absence from his country as much as by his tendency towards obsequiousness in the presence of persons of superior social standing, is dramatically overhauled by Melville when he comes to relate the meetings with Sir John Millet and George III. He seeks instead to convince us of the American patriotism of Israel Potter, a firm believer in his country, trusting in its premises and promises, and looking for guidance from men like Franklin, Jones and Allen who are supposed to be examplars of the American heroic tradition. Apart from his behaviour and stated opinions faced with the presences of Sir John and King George, Potter expressed in his autobiography a sense of weakness of purpose both personally and on behalf of the fighting colonies, even after the Declaration of Independence. At one point he talks of a place "where I might possibly remain confined until America should obtain her independence, or the differences between Great Britain and her American provinces were adjusted." Neither is he always too bold a fellow when faced with armed might. "Indeed," he writes, "a wolf or bear of the American wilderness could not be more terrified or panic stricken at the sight of a firebrand than I then was at that sight of a British Redcoat." Melville does not always feel the need to change drastically remarks such as the last, but he takes great pains to remove any impression of superficiality from the patriotism of Potter.

The real Potter met Sir John Millet, received kindness at his hands, worked well, fed well and was grateful. He refers to him frequently in the narrative as "Sir John," and gives no indication that he ever returned Sir John's kindness with anything other than obedience and loyalty. Melville changes this, and dramatises Israel's instinctive patriotism. Sir John Millet tells Israel that it is obvious that he is American and an escaped prisoner of war:

Old Tombstone Retouched   39

"Mr. Millet," exclaimed Israel aghast, the untasted wine trembling in his hand, "Mr. Millet, I--"

"Mr. Millet--there it is again. Why don't you say <u>Sir John</u> like the rest?"

"Why, sir--pardon me--but somehow, I can't. I've tried; but I can't. You won't betray me for that?"

"Betray--poor fellow! Hark ye, your history is doubtless a secret which you would not wish to divulge to a stranger; but whatever happens to you, I pledge you my honor **I will never betray you.**

"God bless you for that, Mr. Millet."

"Come, come; call me by my right name. I am not Mr. Millet.

<u>You</u> have said <u>Sir</u> to me; and no doubt you have a thousand times said <u>John</u> to other people. Now can't you couple the two? Try once. Come. Only <u>Sir</u> and then <u>John</u>--<u>Sir John</u>--that's all.

"John--I can't--Sir, sir!--your pardon. I didn't mean that " (Ch. IV).

Finally Sir John has to concede to Israel's ingrained patriotism, a power so commanding that it seems to control the motor processes of his speech. Melville has not explained why Sir John had become aware that Israel was an American; he infers that it is a quality that cannot be really concealed. Certainly when Israel meets George, king of England, the latter also received the clear impression that Israel is American. Israel is retreating before the king when "something in his air" catches George's attention:

> "You ain't an Englishman,--no Englishman--no, no. . . You are a Yankee-a Yankee, . . . yes, yes--you are one of that stubborn race,--that very stubborn race."

Melville's King George is a growling, stammering, befuddled old man; Israel is resolute:

40   Melville's ISRAEL POTTER

> "Were you at Bunker Hill?--that bloody Bunker Hill--eh, eh?"
>
> "Yes, sir."
>
> "Fought like the devil--like a very devil, I suppose?"
>
> "Yes, sir."
>
> "Helped flog--helped flog my soldiers?"
>
> "Yes, sir; but very sorry to do it."
>
> "Eh?--eh?--how's that?"
>
> "I took it to be my sad duty, sir."
>
> "Very much mistaken--very much mistaken, indeed. Why do ye sir me?--eh? I'm your king--your king."
>
> "Sir," said Israel firmly, but with deep respect, "I have no king " (Ch. V).

King George does not have Israel apprehended as a rebel or prisoner of war, but mistakes Israel's gratitude for subservience. The American corrects him; he has been conquered "not [by] the king, but the king's kindness."

In so far as Israel Potter is a political work and deals with patriotism, these two meetings with Sir John and King George represent temptations presented to and resisted by the young Israel. Both men represent to Israel opportunity for comfort at the expense of his ideals; he has only to surrender to the political loyalties of either man to alter radically the patterns of flight and poverty marking his life since his entry into Britain. Patriotism is a rewarding virtue only partially: neither man attempts to prosecute Israel, perhaps because they are captivated by his resolution. But they cannot offer him much more while he retains his loyalties. Melville spells out the rewards of compromise, so we know well what Israel has sacrificed is preserving his virgin patriotism even as he feels tempted by the magnaminity of the king:

> Indeed, had it not been for the peculiar

> disinterested fidelity of our adventurer's patriotism, he would soon have sported the red coat; and perhaps under the immediate patronage of his royal friend, been advanced in time to no mean rank in the army of Britain. Nor in that case would we have had to follow him, as at last we shall, through long years of obscure and penurious wandering (Ch. V).

Israel keep this patriotism and places it at the disposal of Franklin and John Paul Jones, and matches it beside that of Ethan Allen. But this is only one aspect of Melville's complex development of a simple story.

By the seventh chapter, where Israel meets Benjamin Franklin, it is clear that Melville has become dissatisfied with the Life and Remarkable Adventures. Potter had met Benjamin Franklin, at least according to his own account; he had also regarded the meeting as a moment of awe and respect for the great man:

> My interview with Doctor Franklin was a pleasing one. For nearly an hour he conversed with me in the most agreeable and instructive manner, listened to the tale of my sufferings with much apparent interest (Life, p. 50).

Melville was not satisfied with this. Melville took an acute interest in the hypothetical response of Franklin to Israel's problems. If Potter could dispose of his meeting with Franklin in a few lines, Melville feels obliged to dwell on the encounter for at least six chapters; by the time Israel is out of Franklin's hands in Melville's story, there is no relationship between the person that Potter met during the revolutionary years and the character constructed out of those few lines by Herman Melville.

Once Melville had made this kind of departure from the Potter narrative, there was to be no return to the close following of the lines of the first six chapters. In fact, there was to be even more pronounced invention. Potter had recorded a meeting with old Benjamin Franklin; he had spoken only in passing of John Paul Jones, perhaps as an exercise in name-dropping, but most certainly never claimed to have met the hero and sailed with him on his campaigns.

> There was no one engaged in the cause of America that did more to establish her fame in England, and to satisfy the high-boasting Britons of the bravery and unconquerable resolution of the Yankees, than the bold adventurer Captain Paul Jones, who for ten or twelve months kept all the western coast of the island in alarm. He boldly landed at Whitehaven, where he burnt a ship in the harbour, and even attempted to burn the town (Life, p. 59).

This was the full extent of Potter's writing concerning John Paul Jones. It triggered in Melville an interest in the captain that covered loosely ten chapters of the novel and led to some of the most distinguished writing of the whole book. Arvin called it the most complex character sketched by Melville between Moby Dick and Clarel.[26]

And if Potter had mentioned Jones without actually meeting him, he neither encountered nor mentioned Ethan Allen. Melville had mentioned him in passing as a paragon of nobility in Pierre: "He who shall be wholly honest, though nobler than Ethan Allen; that man shall stand in danger of the meanest mortal's scorn " (Bk, V, Chap, vii). Melville not only devotes two chapters to Allen, but manages to construct a character of galvanic energy and titanic proportion, a younger Lear whose blasted heath is all of England and her totalitarian processes, and whose rage never declines into madness or simplifies itself into nectarean masochism.

The chapters describing the naval battle between the Serapis and the BonHomme Richard are almost among the finest in the book; hardly inferior are those which find Israel in his own Egyptian bondage, working as a brickmaker near the city of London (Ch. XXIII). To read these passages is to be exposed once again to the Melville who loved Hawthorne's darkness, and whose vision sought out and described with such compulsion scenes of mankind caught at some moment of apocalyptic reflection.[27]

The concern here is with the quality of Melville's writing as he progresses away from the adherence to Potter's tale.

Old Tombstone Retouched   43

There is every indication of growing strength of expression and no sign that Melville's removal from the confines of the Life and Remarkable Adventures was leading to any lack of confidence, reflections of debility or miserable compulsion. The chapter that follows that of the brickmaking scenes, "In The City of Dis," is a splendidly impressionistic rendering of the city of London. Potter had not been dead to the contradictions of the city:

> I found London as it had been represented to me, a large and magnificent city, filled with inhabitants of almost every description and occupation. . . . There is not, perhaps, another city of its size in the whole world, the streets of which display a greater contrast in the wealth and misery, the honesty and knavery of its inhabitants, than the city of London
> (Life, pp. 61-62).

But Melville hardly would have needed to follow Potter's pedestrian and superficial observations; he had himself been in London as a young sailor and as a mature man. Years later, when he came to lecture on the South Seas, he would tell his audiences that "there were two places in the world where man can most effectively disappear--the city of London and the South Seas."[28] And in any event, as Leyda records, Melville was in the fall of 1849 making precisely such notes on London and Paris as he viewed them with an adult and tragic eye. He could never forget "that hereditary crowd--gulfstream of humanity--which, for continuous centuries, has never ceased pouring, like an endless shoal of herring, over London bridge" (Ch. XXIV). Neither did he forget to write in language that showed both the breadth of his vision and the aridity of that desert that was the teeming city of London:

> Whichever way the eye turned, no tree, no speck of any green thing was seen-- no more than in smithies. All laborers, of whatsoever sort, were hued like men in foundries. The black vistas of streets were as the galleries in coal mines; the flagging, as flat as tombstones, ...worn

> heavily down, by sorrowful tramping,
> as the vitreous rocks in the cursed Gal-
> lipagos, over which the convict tortoises
> crawl (Ch. XXIV).

This is all Melville and increasingly magnificent. The Life and Remarkable Adventures, written by an old man returning home and disappointed in his bid to win a pension, and hoping perhaps to recoup some of his losses with a slender volume telling his remarkable story, had long been exhausted as an initiating force for Melville's creative flights. It is true that Melville follows the same path home as did Potter, but even in the final chapter he turns aside, not without patience, from the chafings of an old man who could not or would not understand the workings of the law of the long-deserted land; Melville's hand is still sure as he hastens slowly to the end of Potter's life.

Melville's debt to Potter, then, is a small one. Potter's debt to Melville, if literary immortality is any comfort beyond the grave, is immense. From the point of view of literary excellence, there is nothing remotely remarkable about the Life and Remarkable Adventures. There is evidence to doubt its validity as sincere autobiography; it does not hesitate to employ melodrama to hold attention, or maudlin sentimentality to encourage sympathy. Structurally it is without distinction; its central character invites pity but not admiration; its peripheral figures are faceless sufferers or illdefined agents. If Israel Potter, Melville's eventual creation, has any worth on any level, it is Melville's easy assimilation of the basic framework of the story and the application of his craft to that framework that deserves praise.

Chapter Three

The Monthly Melville

When at last the critic turns to the finished Melville product to understand and evaluate its merit, his initial impression very often is conditioned by the apparent episodic nature of the novel. This is presumably what Arvin means by "a heap of brilliant sketches," and after the first reading we tend to remember Israel and his several encounters as having little semblance of homogeneity. This semblance is further encouraged when it is remembered that Melville wrote the story orginally for the Putnam's Monthly Magazine, and that obviously the serial form demands of an author that each episode should be almost a self-contained world, both summarising swiftly all that has gone before and giving rich promise of events to come; the prime appeal will lie, of course, with each episode being successful in whetting the reader's appetite for more. The magazine origin of Israel Potter should not be ignored; there are obvious signs of its influence on Melville as author. But we do little justice to Melville in presuming that he did not see the work at all times as a whole, unified by theme, character and symbolism.

Putnam's Monthly Magazine played an important part in Melville's career. There is nothing to indicate that the magazine form compromised his ideals as an artist. Before Israel Potter, he had printed in Putnam's both "Bartleby" and the "Encantadas," the first appearing late in 1853 and the latter coming out just before Israel Potter, in the spring of 1854. The "Lightning-Rod Man" completed Melville's publication in that magazine for 1854; the next year, 1855, brought the "Bell Tower" in August, and "Benito Cereno" in October and November. There were other Putnam publications of Melville works. The relationship between the author and his magazine publishers was obviously a mutually satisfactory one; Putnam's had introduced itself to Herman Melville on October 1, 1852 with a circular letter announcing its intention to publish "an Original periodical of a character different from any now in existence," soliciting "an occasional article" from the established author.[1] As for its general quality and reputation once the magazine had begun to flourish, there was the claim that William Makepeace Thackeray had asserted that it was "much the best Mag. in the world,--and was better than Blackwood is or ever was!"[2] It is immaterial whether Thackeray ever made the remark, but it does illustrate the kind of standing enjoyed by Putnam's in the early 1850's. Melville could feel assured of sympathetic editorship in such company.

The circular from Putnam's came at a fortuitous time for Melville, though there were other magazines ready to pay for his material. After Pierre and the general coldness that had greeted Moby Dick, and as Melville's financial problems refused to resolve themselves, the comparatively steady income of the magazines seemed to offer Melville a measure of security and less labor. For Israel Potter Melville received somewhat more than five dollars for every page of manuscript, with Melville retaining the copyright and being paid $100 in advance of publication; these were his own terms, accepted altogether by the magazine.[3] This involvement with the magazine readership had other rewards, as if Melville consciously responded to a more democratically derived audience than that of his earlier novels. This only partially accounts for the changes towards clarity and simplicity in Melville's output, for the important point is that Melville had learnt his lessons from a survey of his mistakes. Even if Melville had not turned to the monthly magazine and had elected instead to try his hand again in the larger field of the novel, it is unlikely that his style would have been in any appreciable way different from that displayed in Putnam's. The magazine was the ideal vehicle for the new restraint and had a bracing effect on Melville's social and financial situation, but it is most likely that style preceded the vehicle in Melville;

faced with the errors of Pierre, Melville had clearly decided that there were certain ways in which he would never again write.

The promise to George Putnam that there would be "nothing of any sort to shock the fastidious" could be adhered to without much difficulty by Melville; the simultaneous promise, however, that "there will be very little reflective writing in it; nothing weighty," was quite another matter. This is not to imply that Melville so abrogated his responsibilities as creator of adventure and interest that he allowed Israel Potter to become a polemical battleground. By "reflective writing" Melville did not mean intellectual content in itself. He was referring to the means he had adopted too often and with too little success in Pierre, of taking the omniscient stance as narrator and launching into the philosophical abstractions or recondite discussions, at times fringing on pedantry, which had been encouraged both by his sense of educational insecurity, his late-discovering mind and his interest in authors such as Burton, who placed great store in the power of the digression. Melville would not admit that these had been largely mistaken discipleships on his part; these digressions still remain "weighty" and "reflective writing" but it is the best guide to his change in thinking that he no longer incorporated them into his work, except with fine circumspection. His only sustained pieces of "omniscient" writing, adopting the editorial rather than pontifical stance, come after the inventive portraits of Franklin, Jones and Allen. All are very well done and have very significant responsibilities: correcting any erroneous impressions of three famous American heroes which might have been caused by the dramatic methods employed in presenting them.

It is very possible that Melville had not anticipated that one day he would depend so much on the monthly magazine. His relationship with Putnam's becomes ironical when one remembers his saucy treatment of the area of publication in Pierre. Pierre is paid several dollars for his sonnets by "the proprietor of that popular periodical, the Gazelle Magazine," and Melville tells us that the editor had never read the sonnets, "but referred them to his professional adviser; and was so ignorant, that, for a long time previous to the periodical's actually being started, he insisted upon spelling the Gazelle with a g for the z" for a ludicrous reason (Bk. XVIII, Chap. II). This was before the publication of Pierre and Melville had doubtless been accosted by publishers of ephemeral magazines from the time of Typee. [4]

48   Melville's ISRAEL POTTER

But perhaps even Melville would have been astonished, if not humbled, by the relationship of fact to invention when lines penned easily in <u>Pierre</u> return only slightly altered a few years later in his own life:

> Upon one occasion, happening suddenly to encounter a literary acquaintance-- a joint editor of the "Captain Kidd Monthly" --who suddenly popped upon him round a corner, Pierre was startled by a rapid-- "Good morning, good morning;-- just the man I wanted:--come, step round now with me, and have your Daguerreotype taken;--get it engraved then in no time --want it for the next issue " (Bk. XVII, Chap. iii).

In May of 1854, George Palmer Putnam writes to Melville:

> We wish very much to have your <u>head</u> as one of our series of portraits . . . Have you not some drawing or daguerreotype that you can lend us ?--Or can you oblige us by having a daguerreotype taken in Pittsfield & let us know <u>the</u> cost, which will be remitted at once?[5]

In spite of the need for holding the monthly interest of the magazine reader and satisfying the promises of restraint made to his editor, Melville did not create anything less than a unified tale reflecting a wide range of his preoccupations and tenuously bound together. By the time the <u>Life and Remarkable Adventures</u> had expended itself, <u>Israel Potter</u> had already pointed in a different direction. Perhaps the main reason why the structural unity of Melville's work has not often been appreciated is that critics have consistently either presumed that unity was deliberately eschewed by Melville in catering to the magazine or, seeking some connective link, have seen their concept founder on this very fact of the episodic construction in the magazine origins of the work. Much more rewarding is a search that seeks not one but two distinct structural patterns, one that would encompass the novel as a finished product, capable of being read, like Poe's ideal poem, at one sitting; the other structural unity would have sought to satisfy the reader of the novel by installment, who, having the span of months between the first few printed pages of the story and the concluding chapter, could not be expected to grasp all symbolic nuances. For unity is as important in a work presented periodically as it is in one available for relatively uninterrupted consumption; the important factor is that these two unities cannot be absolutely identical in the mind of the two types of reader, even though these unities may share vast areas of common ground. The unity demanded by the periodically published story is at once vaguer and more impressionistic than that needed in a complete novel. Symbols of obvious importance in the latter are often weakly apprehended under any other conditions; Melville provides precisely those symbols, but they cannot be isolated from the other, first-occasioned sense of unity that would have been apparent to the readers who brought Putnam's in 1854 and 1855, watching for the Melville train that went by their armchairs only once in every month.

For the monthly reader the structure of Israel Potter might have appeared to resolve itself into three logical divisions. After what must have appeared as general lyrical description of Potter's homeland in the first chapter, the novel is motivated by the picaresque spirit; this first division, apart from the opening chapter, follows closely the letter and line of the Life and Remarkable Adventures; the monthly reader would not have known this, perhaps, but he would have been aware that he was following the story of a man on the run, a man capable of subterfuge and innovation, a young Yankee with native intelligence outwitting the stodgy minds of English folk. Here Melville is doing precisely what he promised in the dedication of the book; he is adhering to the story told by Israel Potter and paying particular attention to fidelity to the narrative. Even those changes in the character of Israel which have been previously noted, particularly the stability of his patriotism, do not affect the picaresque tenor of the novel's first division. And though the phrase certainly overstates the subservience of Melville, those first few chapters (II to VI) may be together called the period of deep dependence, and takes Israel's story up to the meeting with Benjamin Franklin.

The break is not abrupt. When Potter had something to say in the Life and Remarkable Adventures, Melville was listening and willing to pass the word on; when Potter ceased to be interesting, and when the vicarious bond between the old soldier and Melville was too strained by the actions and opinions of the former, Melville abandoned the tale in the interest of his own critical and artistic integrity. This departure came at the mid-point of the Life and Remarkable Adventures, and leaves comparatively untouched the details of Potter's suffering and the deprivations of London life. Potter's original story was badly imbalanced between adventure on the one hand and misery on the other; Melville sought after a more sensible distribution. There has been a tendency to see Melville, burdened with the unhappiness of his own life, unable to relate the misery which the old man had faced. Thus Matthiessen writes of Melville:

> When he came to the ex-soldier's destitution in London, his own sense of suffering was so great that he could not bear to dwell on Potter's, and slurred over what was to have been his main subject in a couple of short chapters. [6]

This is a questionable conclusion; there is no evidence that Melville ever intended anything more than he actually did, just as there is no indication that what he did was insufficient. There was less to Potter's catalogue of assorted suffering than appeared at first glance; Melville obviously knew the book thoroughly after having it for at least four years; when he turned away from it in his own novel, it was with the best and most premeditated of intentions. Melville's deviations even in the earlier sections have been noted already in the case of the meeting with King George, where he transformed an innocuous, name-dropping event into a nationalistic confrontation between a stammering king who senses Israel's Americanness the way a dog scents a trail, and in the embellishment of the meeting between Israel and Sir John Millet, where, in the face of danger, Melville had Israel refusing to adopt the language of obeisance. These have been the principal indicators of Melville's discontent with the narrative; by the time he comes to the meeting with Ben Franklin, he is away on his own.

The second section of Israel Potter is marked by the rise and dominance of the comic method, and follows Israel from the meeting with Doctor Franklin through the return to Squire Woodcock's, the incarceration in the cell in the Woodcock home, and the escape and union with John Paul Jones; it continues through the campaign of Jones in the Irish sea, but dies swiftly away, never to return, once the battle between the Serapis and the Bon

Homme Richard had been joined. There is a deceptive lightness of tone in the chapter following the great battle, "The Shuttle"; it is only too apparent that what we are seeing here, in Israel's wandering about the vast city of a battleship, is, in part, an epitomising of his rootlessness, a prefiguring of his approaching desolation and rejection by the people both of his native land and of England. This would have been known to the monthly reader; Melville had announced Israel's eventual rejection as early as the end of his first chapter. But between Franklin's first appearance and the great battle, the dominant tone is satirical; it is uppermost in the characterization of Franklin and merges not unhappily with broad farce in Israel's flight from the Woodcock home dressed in the Squire's clothes and terrifying the household before he is himself petrified by what turns out to be a scarecrow. This is the book's middle passage, and Melville's. If the atmosphere is at times a trifle inebriate, it could be that Melville is celebrating his emancipation from the words and thoughts of old Israel himself. The spectacle of his close adherence to the text of a story uttered by a senile veteran and penned probably in haste by some hack could not have been a pleasant one for Herman Melville. Here in the second part of Israel Potter Melville moves out on his own. This is one of the great moments of Melville's career. It is the time of his first generous release of his imagination and skill, along the proportions to which he had been previously accustomed, since Pierre had come to its dismal end. What sparked the new vitality in Melville cannot be precisely computed; but once this initial levity is spent, it proves to have been the precursor of an even more recognisable Melville; with the battle between the ships, Melville loses interest in the satiric and, as the battle progresses and the carnage grows, moves steadily towards the third and final portion of the book.

There is no mistaking the note that enters the book once the two ships approach each other for the battle; yet, it comes as a shock when, in Chapter XIX, Melville turns from describing Jones' erratic gallivanting up and down the high seas and his farcical attempt to burn the ships at Whitehaven, as well as his mock-heroic assault on the castle of the Earl of Selkirk. As the Serapis and Bon Homme Richard approach, Melville sounds the first disquieting notes, ending the light and mocking tone in which he had up to this point related the various battles and encounters of John Paul Jones. For the first time since the overture of the first chapter, Melville dwells on the long descriptive passage replete with metaphor and simile and sustained by its own opulence and power:

> Not long after, an invisible hand came and set down a great yellow lamp in the east. The hand reached up unseen from below the horizon, and set the lamp down right on the rim of the horizon, as on a threshold.... The lamp was the round harvest moon; the one solitary foot-light of the scene. But scarcely did the rays from the lamp pierce that languid haze. Objects before perceived with difficulty, now glimmered ambiguously. Bedded in strange vapors, the great footlight cast a dubious, half-demoniac glare across the waters, like the phantasmagoric stream sent athwart a London flagging in a night-rain rom an apothecary's blue and green window (Ch. XIX).

This is a fine stroke, deeply impressive even on the monthly reader. Searching for a simile, Melville has blended the moon-lit sea with the Gothic terror of a London night; Israel's fate is pre-figured, even at his moment of epic heroism at the side of John Paul Jones. And at the end of the battle Melville confirms the impression that this has been an emotional and artistic watershed for him and for the book; he does not make any attempt to glorify the day's deeds, or heap honors on the American victors. From this point on there is no turning back either to the comic spirit or to the relinquishing of the narrative assignment to Potter's shaky old hands. After his sojourn on board the British battleship, Israel returns to England to find Ethan Allen in captivity. Next he finds himself in the brickyard near London, in the city of Dis, buffeted by Fate, haunted by hallucination:

> And so, Israel, now an old man, was bewitched by the mirage of vapors; he had dreamed himself home into the mists of the Housatonic mountains; ruddy boy on the upland pastures again (Ch. XXV).

Finally he goes home with his son; his family is gone, and so are his chances for a pension; eventually, he dies.

This tripartite division of the book is almost as logical and apparent as it is convenient. The evolving serial form of the novel from summer of 1854 to the spring of the following year could not conceal the blossoming unity of the work from the opening felicity of its nature description, through the excitement of the elusive Israel, relieved by the lightness and deftness of Melville's humor, and resolving swiftly and irrevocably into the darker seriousness that brings the novel home with honors into the Melville canon. This is no heap of brilliant sketches but a brilliant and methodical development of theme and characterisation through the medium of the incident. The separate qualities of adventure, comedy and tragedy all need to be examined against the total work and the patterns of all of the Melville's writing, but they do not stand apart in the novel as occasional offerings randomly flung from the pen of an erratic genius.

And yet such a division of the work hardly does it justice; it barely repudiates the notion of shallowness, of a lack of important purpose or intellectual content; it simply is inadequate as a final accounting of Melville's art in Israel Potter. It is the means by which he satisfied his commitment to George Palmer Putnam, and the reason why the various reviews of each installment generally were enthusiastic in encouraging reading of the sequences. But it is simply not enough for any lofty placement of Israel Potter among the list of Melville's works. Professor Farnsworth comes close to the core of the problem surrounding Israel Potter with his passing remark that "One suspects that Israel Potter is not as anomalous in the Melville canon as it has often been treated."[7] For while we look for the new in the novel, for signs of a real progression in the art of Melville, it is first necessary to place the work close to the heartland of Melville in order to avoid the popular impression, questioned by Farnsworth, that it is a bastard product of Melville's "illegitimate" relationship with the magazines, with a doubtful patrimony because of the debt to the Life and Remarkable Adventures.

Such a close relationship to the heartland of Melville and to Melville's personal life-experience, so often found missing by critics except in the largely irrelevant sense of fellow-sufferers, is discernible in Israel Potter. For what probably most fascinated Melville when he at last turned to write his novel was not the opportunity to engage in descriptions of picaresque incidents or even the chance to try his hand at retelling the battles of John Paul Jones (these were all basically derivative in origin), but instead the possibility of alternative response to the problems that had faced Potter and the problems that faced Melville during those wintry years after the writing of *Pierre*. His concern was not only with the problems, but with the responses to the problems. By the time he has examined the varieties of response, he has arrived at conclusions not only about his own trials and attitudes but also about similar confrontations at the national and universal levels.

It was hardly the first time that Melville had interested himself in the possibilities of alternative response. In *Moby Dick*, the golden doubloon is variously interpreted; in the novel, the challenge of the great white whale is a variety of things to the seemingly infinite variety of men on board the *Pequod*. The responses of the three harpooners are a unified and scintillating professionalism, comparatively free of reflection; to Starbuck, the task is an unholy one anathematized by his conviction that a monomaniacal pursuit of a mysterious whale is the pursuit of self-destruction: heroic valor must be tempered by almost spiritual discretion. To Ahab, of course, all of life as the oppressor finds its apotheosis in the malevolence of the circum-terrestrial and deep-diving whale; Ahab makes the only response he finds admissible: total commitment to the eradication of that evil force.

But it is possible to see the pursuit of Moby Dick by the *Pequod*, and the pursuit of *Moby Dick*, the novel, by Herman Melville, as the chasing of a primarily abstract obsession both for the character in the work, Ahab, and the author of the work itself, Herman Melville. In *Moby Dick*, Melville was seeking metaphysical explanations for the undefined dilemma of life as he had till then known it; there is the implicit conviction that the wholly heroic response is not altogether adequate because, on that battleground where human aspiration and ambition meet and attempt to conquer the vicissitudes of life, the highest ground, the totally impregnable positions, are held by those same metaphysical absolutes that are extra-societal and incapable both of resolution and defeat.

Mardi represents Melville's premature attempt to delineate artistically the lines of this conflict between human response and untouchable absolute. It failed principally because the book, as in the case of *Pierre*, had been inadequately motivated by Melville's own personal experience; he was unable to bridge the gap between the historical phenomena that constituted his experience of life and the metaphysical speculation and suspicion spawned from reflection on those phenomena. In writing Mardi Melville indicated that he was insufficiently educated in the relationship between personal experience and the growth of meaningful symbolic utterance; his creative act of heresy was his implied insistence that faith in intuition, without the observation and experience of humanity at work, could lead to creative salvation. With the collapse of Mardi's confabulated superstructure, Melville had to retrace his life through the initiation and sufferings of Redburn and Whitejacket before he was finally ready for another foray into the philosophical abstractions of human response; by this time he had learnt that even the most tortured allegory depends for its artistic success on the ability of the narrative to suggest to the reader a physically verifiable alternative, and one that is almost immediately perceptible if that reader is at all sympatheic and educated in the commonplaces of western symbolism. It was a lesson that Melville had once again to apply after Pierre.

And if Ahab represents the apex of defiance as a response to real or imagined evil, it is obvious that by the time Melville had written "Bartleby the Scrivener" he was genuinely interested in, and perhaps even fascinated by, the possibilities of an antipodal attitude: the potentiality of non-response, of true passive resistance. Bartleby is the direct opposite of Ahab; moreover, the arena of his engagement with the world-opposition is neither in the airy fantasising of Mardi or the heroically realized whalehunting of the Pequod in Moby Dick. Bartleby's world and Herman Melville's world were contiguous and contemporaneous and realistically drawn. Bartleby and Melville take the concept of non-response to its logical conclusion, scorning not only the threatening gestures of evil, but also the benevolent postures of traditional virtues and kindness. At the end, when Bartleby is finally asleep with kings and counsellors after turning a deaf ear to lesser men, Melville seems to be aware that there has been something unsatisfactory about his response. Its greatest benefit has been perhaps in its lesson to like the lawyer, who for the first time realizes that there can be more to life than the mere acceptance of compromise as the over-riding arbitrator of human complexity. The disquiet that the lawyer feels in the company of this rigid non-acceptance makes him, if not a "better" man, at least a person more aware of that complexity in life and of the flexibility of the human spirit in its death struggle with the world and its economic, spiritual and societal snares.

In the "Encantadas," too, Melville is more fascinated ultimately not by the islands' geographical eccentricities as much as by the varieties of human response occasioned by those strange deserts in the beautiful Pacific. The stoicism of Hunilla reflects the non-response of Bartleby, although there is an important difference between the two: that Hunilla lives by hope for a better life, while Bartleby dies through despair. As for the "Encantadas" and Israel Potter, both works were designed along episodic lines; both are attempts at depersonalization of Melville's literary efforts, and both became more than they originally promised because of Melville's compulsion towards the depiction of character and personality, and his conviction that life's significance is best observed in the response of the individual to the challenge of existence, and not simply through observation of flora and fauna in reaction to earthly phenomena, as in the first sketches of the "Encantadas." Thus, by the eighth sketch, Melville gravitates towards human flesh and blood in its classic Melvillean confrontation, facing the ruthlessness and predictable perversion of life. But long before this he has evinced interest in another kind of response, the animal responses of the great tortoises to their eternal co-existence with these islands of death, "fixed, cast, glued into the very body of cadaverous death" (Sketch 1). Hunilla, Oberlus and others have their response to the islands and the tortoises have yet another, complete and hopeless surrender:

> For, apart from their strictly physical features, there is something strangely self-condemned in the appearance of these creatures. Lasting sorrow and penal hopelessness are in no animal form so suppliantly expressed as in theirs; while the thought of their wonderful longevity does not fail to enhance the impression (Sketch 1).

Israel Potter at one point will almost succumb to this response and surrender completely; in real life, he seemed to have come closer to it than Melville allowed his fictional counterpart. Melville submerges the forty years in England as soon as we have seen Israel almost trapped in the world of "penal hopelessness"; Melville surely had precisely these tortoises in mind when he wrote "Bartleby," for Bartleby is a great tortoise self-condemned in a world which he doubtless regards as an intolerable and barren travesty of the ideal to which man can only aspire and never attain. Bartleby and the tortoises are not incapable of other response; they have merely finally concluded that there is no other eternally viable procedure in facing the world. For the tortoises are portrayed by Melville not as unfeeling brutes without a great history, but instead as survivors of great battles, veterans of great wars, heirs to some tradition like the whales of Moby Dick; they are veterans in the same way that Israel Potter, having fought at Bunker Hill and with John Paul Jones, is a veteran, and they bear their scars from their engagements as noticeably as Israel bears his. They are:

> black as widower's weeds, heavy as chests of plate, with vast shells medallioned and orbed like shields, and dented and blistered like shields that have breasted a battle . . . (Sketch 2).

They bear scars, too, from their absolute inflexibility, as Bartleby eventually dies from this inflexible refusal to compromise with the world. Just as the tortoises "ran themselves heroically against rocks, and long abide there, nudging, wriggling, wedging in order to displace them, and so hold on their inflexible path, so does Bartleby try to hold his course and dies in the bargain, "their crowning curse is their drudging impulse to straight forwardness in a belittered world." The obduracy of the tortoises has its impact on Melville just as the steadfastness or Bartleby educates the lawyer:

> With them I lost myself in volcanic mazes, brushed away endless boughs of rotting thickets; till finally in a dream I found myself sitting cross-legged upon the foremost, a Brahmin similarly mounted upon either side, froming a tripod of foreheads which upheld the universal cope (Sketch 2).

Melville informs us that there are two sides to the tortoise; there are, then, two sides to humanity, and Hunilla is the bright side. She represents the step away from the despair of the tortoise and Bartleby, but she is not the only other possible response. Melville examines others: Oberlus, for example, has his own ideas about the application of solitary defiance to all that is reprehensible to his unfortunate mind. He meets fire with fire; if the world to him is venemous, he neither drops quietly out, as Bartleby does, not sits steadfastly in, as Hunilla elects to do in order to change her lot in the world which appears to have forsaken her. Oberlus in his response is not unlike Ahab, anxious to strike back and destroy that which seeks to destroy him; he has no misguided ideal driving him, however, and a poor sense of style; "while planting, his whole aspect and all his gestures were so malevolently and uselessly sinister and secret, that he seemed rather in the act of dropping poison into wells rather than potatoes into soil" (Sketch 9). He turns his back to many a stranger on first meeting him, "possibly, because that was his better side, since it revealed the least."

Oberlus' defiance itself is a progression away from total abjuring personified in Bartleby and the wistful acceptance of fate by the Chola widow, Hunilla. In the seventh sketch of the Encantadas we meet yet another variety of response, and it is one that finds man not only repelling man but also defying the traditional hierarchy to establish liaisons with animals of the earth, over which man had traditionally held lordship. The Creole comes to Charles' Island as ruler,

> accompanied, strange to say, by a disciplined cavalry company of large, grim dogs. These, it was observed on the passage, refusing to consort with the emigrants, remained aristocratically grouped around their master on the elevated quarter-deck, casting disdainful glances forward at the inferior rabble there (Sketch 7).

The monarchical aspirations of the Creole, who wishes to be made "Supreme Lord of the Island, one of the princes of the powers of the earth," exacerbates a sin he has already committed, turning away from hope in fellow humanity to the alliance with animals. The Creole has made his irrevocable judgment about the individual and his potential, about the nature of the correct political process, about adversity and man's recourse in fighting this adversity. In the end, the dogs and the Creole fight the humans in a bloody battle on the beach that ends in defeat for the Creole and his canine clique. Balance and harmony are restored only after that defeat and the Creole's suing for peace. The concept of man allied with beast, or imitating the action of the tiger in time of peace as well as war, is part of the investigation of the potential varieties of response that Melville explores on other planes in Israel Potter.

Hunilla is indeed the bright side of the tortoise and Melville is not so gloomy to treat her story with scant regard. She is the bright side not because she spectacularly evinces a high regard for the most positive elements of life, but because she is steadfast in quiet conviviality. Perhaps Melville is saying that this is as far as mankind can go in positively adopting the world as a companion, for he has pity and sympathy for Bartleby but nothing more positive; Bartleby is exposed as a case history, a demonstration of what life can do to a man who is good. Hunilla does not have the means to take up arms and yet refuses to be conquered. Abandoned whether through malice or misfortune by a captain contracted to return for her, she persists in her faith:

> "The ship sails this day, today," at last said Hunilla to herself; "this gives me certain time to stand on; without certainty I go mad. In loose ignorance I have hoped and hoped; now in firm knowledge I will but wait. Now I live and no longer perish in bewilderings. Holy Virgin, aid me!" (Sketch 8).

Hunilla has not come to this state without great effort; having counted out her days on the piece of reed that supports her, she can count no more; only with great effort does she brace herself behind her faith. Melville salutes her, for she has achieved for herself what so many of the dead letters in the Dead Letter office in Washington, where Bartleby had once worked, fail to do for those human casualties who "died despairing," or "died unhoping," or "died stifled by unrelieved calamities. On errands of life, these letters speed to death." Melville ends chiding Bartleby and that despairing element of humanity. There is another side he tells us, represented by the Hunillas of the world: "Humanity, thou strong thing, I worship thee, not in the laureled victor, but in this vanquished one." Hunilla is only temporarily vanquished; at the point where others bow out, she draws herself up to the full measure of man. Deluded Israel never matches Hunilla; he only survives and learns his lesson when it is too late and his life is all but over. But "in the city of Dis" he has a chance to make the same resolution; the flagging in the streets of that city, London, are "worn heavily down, by sorrowful tramping, as the vitreous rocks in the cursed Gallipagos, over which the convict tortoises crawl." Melville consciously pursues the picture of London as akin to the Encantadan wasteland. The "Encantadas" are "five-and-twenty heaps of cinder" and "a group rather of extinct volcanoes than of isles;" the city of London is "this cindery City of Dis," a place where the air is darkened as if "some neighbouring volcano. . . were about to whelm the great town " (Ch. XXIV). Israel does not subvert the standards of humanity, as the Creole does, or turn aside and die with Bartleby. Indecisive to the end, having no real personal standards which can assist him in time of need, his course remains erratic. "Not by constitution disposed to gloom," he kept searching for some way out; however, inept his searchings, "stoic influences were at work." But here perversity sets in. For where Hunilla's stoicism eventually rescued her from the isles, Israel's "stoic influences" merely preserve him for greater miseries,

> when by sickness, destitution, each busy ill of exile, he was destined to experience a fate, uncommon even to luckless humanity -- a fate whose crowning qualities were its remoteness from relief and its depth of obscurity -- London, adversity, and the sea, three Armageddons, which, at one and the same time, slay and secrete their victims (Ch. XXIV).

Three Armageddons: London, adversity and the sea. In the cases of Bartleby, Hunilla, Oberlus, the Creole, Ahab, Starbuck and the adventurers of Mardi, as well as in other aspects of Melville's writing that saw humans searching for a role of defiance of compromise, there is not in general a multiplicity of opposition. One of the masterstrokes of Moby Dick, already discussed in part, is that Ahab convincingly localizes his antipathies in the physical being of one whale, and that Melville is able, most notably through his passages on cetology, to imbue the whale with such degrees of heritage and honor that it becomes a fitting and equal antagonist for Ahab and not a pathetic figure persecuted by an evil old man. Wellingborough Redburn has two arenas of struggle; faced with the city and the sea, both for the first time, he emerges from both experiences a wiser person, led to a greater degree of realization because he has been carried along by the current of his innocence without being able or willing to drop out of the race, as Bartleby does, or develop an animus such as Ahab's, or even articulate a quiet optimism in the manner of Hunilla.

By the time Melville came to write Israel Potter, however, he had developed the clearest picture he had ever had of what really constitutes the evil that distends the human soul and the hidden reefs on which ambition and virtue founder. Perhaps heightened because of his experience with his government and the disappointment over the consulship, perhaps because of the storm-warnings in the Union in the decade of the 1850's, he had come to a clearer awareness of the role of the nation in the development of personality. The artistic, psychological and social pressures which attended his life after Pierre could only have had an accelerating influence on any drift in his life towards a more conservative point of view. More importantly as far as his art was concerned, Melville must have begun to render the struggle not always in metaphysical terms between almost mythical forces of evil exemplified in some character's mind's eye, but of a highly tangible, more secular, presence in such day-to-day realities as the regimen of the lawyer's office, the four walls of the soulless office, the emasculating threat of the newly mechanised world. In "The Tartarus of Maids"

> machinery--that vaunted slave of humanity--here stood menially served by human beings, who served mutely and cringingly as the slave serves the Sultan. The girls did not so much seem accessory wheels to the general machinery as mere cogs to the wheels.

This economic investigation of at least one part of a larger mental and social malaise denotes the distance Melville has travelled away from the mythopoeic background of Mardi or the Byronic

Romanticism of Taji and Tommo.

This is to suggest, then, that far from being a painfully desolate historical novel or a brilliant heap of sketches of an enjoyable but trivial work, Melville's Israel Potter is a cold, hard book; its episodic structure, its satire and its farce, its swashbuckling adventure and picaresque vignettes are all part of the book, but not its dominant features. It is a cold, hard book because in it Melville addresses himself to problems that for him were real and urgent, and which, at one time or another, had been of dominant importance in his life. Moreover, he comes to deal with these problems not at a time or artistic indecision, as is so often urged, but at a time when his control was never greater and when his philosophical positions had lost initial enthusiasms in favor of more informed opinion. What is partly unfolded in Israel Potter is Melville's evaluation of a variety of ways of life, including, in his case, the several roads not taken. One by one, in the portraits of Israel himself, Benjamin Franklin, John Paul Jones and Ethan Allen, Melville measures these routes through his manipulation of the historical truths recorded concerning each personage. It is in the observations of these manipulations that the greater rewards of the novel, beyond the vicarious thrill of pubescent adventure, deliver themselves. Potter, Franklin, Jones and Allen—each typifies a kind of response to the Armageddons of life. It is clear that Melville identifies his own choice most of all with that of Potter, a victim as much of fate as of his own indecisions and irresolution, an errand-boy of Fate serving in the shadow of men who approach the coming battles either with a conceived plan or a fiery purpose. It is equally clear that Franklin's response is not attractive in his eyes, and that Melville "recoils from Benjamin Franklin as from a model of successful Philistinism."[8] John Paul Jones represents an advance over the coy, crass and crafty opportunist that Franklin seems to be; he espouses Franklin's philosophy while tempering it with dynamic action and a tempestuous imagination and soul. If Franklin was "everything but a poet," in Melville's words, in Jones "there was a bit of a poet as well as the outlaw," and for Melville, that had made all the difference. Ethan Allen, however, knew neither the craftiness of Franklin nor the compromise of Jones; his, in Melville's view, was the purest spirit.

He had been able to thunder out his repudiation of all that was repulsive to his great soul. For Jones, revolt was as much a game as an enterprise of honor. For Franklin, in Melville's caricature, expediency and pettiness secured all things. For Israel Potter, life was a danger in which the face of timidity was excusable and valor always qualified by discretion.

For Melville, this trinity of Armageddons which Israel faces at the end of his running had been the reality of his life and also of his work. London, adversity and the sea represented the great battlegrounds on which Melville had fought; by London, of course, Melville meant the interaction and stresses of the urban environment in contrast to the bucolic peace of Pittsfield where he was content to pass most of the time. Melville abhorred the city in one of the contradictions of his democratic philosophy; he might have been a "ruthless democrat," but he turned aside in terror from the spectacle of man gathered in multitudes in one great camp. Cities stole the souls of men, made them individually and collectively less than human, deprived them of dignity. Israel stands on London bridge to watch the "gulf-stream of humanity, . . . an endless shoal of herring," swirl by helplessly, "knowing not who they were; never destined, it may be, to behold them again; one after the other, they drifted by, uninvoked ghosts from Hades." The city destroyed not only man, but also nature; it was a self destruction, because the city was man congregational; " The Thames, which far away, among the green fields of Berks, ran clear as a brook, here, polluted by continual vicinity to man, curdled on between rotten wharves, one murky sheet of sewerage" (Ch. XXIV). In Pierre, as the three unfortunates enter the city in exile, Isabel wonders why the wheels of the coach are making a new, more ominous sound:

> "The Pavements, Isabel; this is the town."
> Isabel was silent.
> But, for the first time for many weeks, Delly voluntarily spoke:
> "It feels not so soft as the green sward, Master Pierre."
> "No, Miss Ulver," said Pierre, very bitterly, "the buried hearts of some dead citizens have perhaps come to the surface."
> "Sir?" said Delly.
> "And are they so hard-hearted here?" asked Isabel.

> "Ask yonder pavements, Isabel. Milk dropped from the milkman's can in December, freezes not more quickly on those stones, than does snow-white innocence, if in poverty, it chance to fall in these streets" (Book XVI, Chap. i).

One senses that the city aggravated Bartleby's sickness; the city contracts itself about the sufferer until a shared room becomes microcosmic of all the amoral promiscuity of the urban situation; if Israel Potter could list crime after crime encouraged by city life in the <u>Life and Remarkable Adventures</u>, Wellingborough Redburn had sampled city grotesquerie with his young and horrified eyes in Liverpool.

The antithesis of the city is the sea; it is an Armageddon, too, a place where the forces of good and evil meet to do battle and where souls are won and lost; it is also a consolation for the land-weary. Life in the city is almost intolerable; flight from the city to the hermitage in the forest, Melville tells us, is "the refuge of the narrow-minded misanthrope; a hammock on the ocean is the asylum for the generous distressed" (Ch. II). As <u>Moby Dick</u> opens, Ishmael commends the sea as the escape from the murderous grip of city life; in fact, the urge towards the sea is deep in the soul of man, whether or not it is openly recognised:

> Circumambulate the city of a dreamy Sabbath afternoon... What do you see? -- Posted like silent sentinels all around the town, stand thousands upon thousands of mortal men fixed in ocean reveries. Some leaning against the spiles; some seated upon the pier-heads; some looking over the bulwarks of ships from China;... But these are all landsmen; of week days pent in lath and plaster -- tied to counters, nailed to benches, clinched to desks. How then is this? Are the green fields gone? What do they here? (Ch. I).

The truth is that some, like Ishmael, seek solace in the ocean from those dull November days of the soul, lad "with lean brow and hollow eye; given to unseasonal meditativeness"(Ch. XXXV); others reap the almost voluntary harvests of the ocean, like Starbuck, gathering what is rightfully theirs because God has given them dominion over the creatures of the sea. But the sea has its sanctity, symbolic of purity as all water is, and both the "sunken eyed young Platonist" and the reaper of the ocean's harvest cannot violate this sanctity. The ocean, in Melville, will not tolerate those who turn those great commons into private or public battlegrounds for their monomaniacal obsessions, as with Ahab, or their intestinal feuds, as encouraged by John Paul Jones. Jones takes the initiative in a battle that Melville described vividly and excitingly but never enthusiastically in terms of honor, for it is dishonorable. Caught in the heat of battle, "Paul flew hither and thither like the meteoric corposant-ball, which shiftingly dances on the tips and verges of ships' rigging in storms." His blue tattooing, seen by battlelight, is "cabalistically terrific as the charmed standard of Satan." After the bitterly fought engagement, "the Richard, gorged with slaughter, wallowed heavily, gave a long roll, and blasted by tornadoes of sulphur, slowly sunk, like Gomorrah, out of sight" (Ch. XIX). The Bon Homme Richard sinks like the Biblical city of sin, but the sea has proven to be capable of its own swift and terrible punishment, reflecting in its own character the duality of good and evil. It, too, pursues its victims who challenge its hegemony; it is capable of pacific friendship and hellish vengeance, and the water between the two thundering ships is a "Lethean canal-- pond-like in its smoothness compared with the sea without," into which the sinners from both ships fall and are carried away, lost forever. Does the sea sometime lure susceptible man to his death? Is it as vicious as the city itself, a Scylla to which foolish humanity comes in retreat from the Charybdis of the city?

> It was about eight o'clock at night that this strange quarrel was picked in the middle of the ocean. Why cannot men be peaceable on that great common? Or does nature in those fierce night-brawlers, the billows, set mankind but a sorry example? (Ch. XX).

It is the sea, the great Atlantic, that stands obdurately between Israel and his homeland; once upon a time, a sea parted before a great moral and religious presence to save a whole people from the wrath of Pharoah's army, then destroyed that army more in vengeance than of necessity; it would not do the same for this Israel. In his hallucination of July, 1800 (Ch. XXV) Israel dreams himself at home with Old Huckleberry, his mother's favorite pillion horse, as he tends the grassy oval in St. James Park; "but soon stopping midway, and forlornly gazing round at the enclosure, he bethought him that a far different oval, the great oval of the sea, must be crossed ere his crazy errand could be done." Israel can dream of home and talk of home to his son, but the mighty presence of the ocean stands between dreams and reality.

And whatever part of his life was untouched by the arms of London and the sea certainly was no stranger to adversity. The early years of ease and even luxury to which he had become accustomed had given way, after the bankruptcy and eventual death of his father, to a decade of financial insecurity, second-class education and even down-right deprivation. His initial sailing trips had been a rude awakening to the realities of vice and inhumanity; his whaling experience could hardly have restored his confidence in the efficacy of the genteel life for which his birth had seemed to prepare him. In fact, to Israel and to Melville, adversity may have been the crucial and pervasive Armageddon; at that moment when the individual is faced with an immovable object or an irresistible force comes the challenge and the demands for response. Mardi had been representative of that adversity, when the failure of a major effort threatened Melville's career and his newly adopted livelihood and raised questions about his potential, whether or not he was really meant to go down to posterity only as a " man who lived among the cannibals. "[9] Or when the consulship had been refused, or Pierre failed, or during the adverse times of young Melville's initiation into the sea-going fraternity. For Israel and for Melville that particular Armageddon of adversity had proved a shifting and unpredictable venue: it encompassed in its physical manifestation both London and the sea. For Franklin and Allen, the sea had no special connotation and no one knows what London meant to Jones in Melville's peculiar definition of his character, but they all faced in Israel Potter the overwhelming challenge of adversity, and each chooses his own weapons. Melville's main artistic responsibility was the unifying of these three Armageddons and responses into a complex whole; the book that was eventually published early in July of 1855, had to be greater than the sum of those parts which appeared once a month in the pages of Putnam's Monthly Magazine.

Chapter Four

Broadcloth and Linsey-Woolsey

What kind of book is Israel Potter? It is many things: biography, historical fantasy, legitimate historical piece, farce, tragedy, social and political satire. Into what genre, then, does this work fall? The critic fails by under estimating Melville's willingness to reach back over the centuries for masters and models.

Spenser, Shakespeare, Sir Thomas Browne, Milton and Robert Burton are most often listed as influences. Less appreciated has been Melville's reading in medieval literature and his exploitation of materials from not only the writings of the greatest of the medievalists, Chaucer and Dante, but from lesser poets; even less recognized has been Melville's assimilation of devices, attitudes, themes and genres most popular in the Middle Ages. There is need for further study of the role of Dante Alighieri, through the Divine Comedy, in the shaping of Melville's craft. How profound was Melville's assimilation of Cary's famous translation of Dante's major work, which Melville bought in the summer of 1848 and read thoroughly? I suggest only the most modified influence of the Divine Comedy on Israel Potter; however modified that influence, it is indispensable to our appreciation of Melville's work and to its ultimate admittance into the general medieval literary setting where it is most comfortable.

68   Melville ISRAEL POTTER

Dante and Shakespeare were both major influences on Pierre; though Hamlet is obvious, the Divine Comedy weighed heavily on Pierre and Melville. Indeed, perhaps nowhere else in all of Melville is there such explicit acknowledgement of the influence of a specific author. In his first major soliloquy we are introduced to Pierre's involvement with the Italian: "Dante! Night's and Hell's poet he. No we will not open Dante... Francesca's mournful face is now ideal to me. Flaxman might evoke it wholly--make it present in lines of misery--bewitching power. No! I will not open Flaxman's Dante. Damned be the hour I read in Dante" (Book II, Ch. 7). In that soliloquy or reverie under the pine tree, Pierre's outburst against Dante was a fit of impatience against "the one who, in a former time, had first opened to his shuddering eyes the infinite cliffs and gulfs of human mystery and misery" (Book III, Ch. 3). When Pierre turns to writing his great work, the Inferno, along with Hamlet, serves as a guide. Charles Millthorpe sees him as being "in the Inferno dream," and wonders whether he is "going to paint and illustrate the Inferno" as he writes the work.

And later Melville editorializes:

> The man Dante Alighieri received unforgivable affronts and insults from the world; and the poet Dante Alighieri bequeathed his immortal curse to it, in the sublime malediction of the Inferno. The fiery tongue whose political forking lost him the solacements of this world, found its malicious counterpart in that muse of fire, which would forever bar the vast bulk of mankind from all solacement in the worlds to come. Fortunate for the felicity of the Dilettante in Literature, the horrible allegorical meanings of the Inferno, lie not on the surface.

This superficial glance at Dante and the Divine Comedy in Pierre is clear evidence that Melville was well aware of Dante's accomplishment in allegory, of the tradition of the medieval poem and of the enormous potential available in the yoking of seemingly disparate material. Part of Melville's floundering in Pierre is also directly traceable to the influence of Dante; Melville's attempt at exploiting an ironic counterpoint to the progression of the young searcher-after-truth, not rising like Dante to the beatific vision but sinking instead into the morass of human disillusionment; Pierre's flight towards the corrupting city and his Dantesque vision of Enceladus and the rising of the Titans. In Israel Potter, he found a more sympathetic base; he also demonstrated a greater discrimination and economy in borrowing from Dante or anyone. His description of London, boldy entitled "In The City of Dis" demonstrates his inculcations from Dante; there is even evidence of Melville's reading in some of Dante's own sources, the sixth book of the Aeneid and the eleventh book of the Odyssey; if old Israel looks at times like Lear or Oedipus, there are also similarities to Virgil's portrait of Anchises in the sixth book of Aeneid.

It would be an error to superimpose Dante's progressions in the Inferno on Israel's flight towards Melville's City of Dis; there are too many other elements in Israel Potter. I have attempted to establish an empathy between Melville's Dante, along with a suggestion that Melville worked in "the medieval vein." Such a phrase is difficult to define, and yet, in Melville's case, it amounts only to an understanding of the major artistic conventions of Dante and his followers, admiration for their achievements, and some practice in the adaptation of these lessons to Melville's own interests and capabilities. Before Israel Potter, he had opportunity for such practice as late as Pierre.

While the question of the specific genre of Israel Potter remains unanswered there is some difficulty in making any kind of claim for the work as an artistic product. The answer perhaps lies in a combination of genres, with all drawn from traditions popular in the medieval setting and unified by an appreciation of such a setting. One author faced with the same problems (or ambitions) as Melville was William Langland, the reputed author of Piers Ploughman; I am not suggesting any similarity in scope or subject, but only that Langland and Melville were both working within medieval literary traditions and both found problems of accommodation because of their multiplicity of purpose within those traditions. Professor M.W. Bloomfield in his Piers Plowman As A Fourteenth-Century Apocalypse (New Brunswick, New Jersey, 1961) has summarised Langland's distress: "Actually, it seems that Langland never could decide what form he was using, and from beginning to end, part of the difficulty of Piers to its readers is its confusion of genres. Just as Langland could never come to rest in his search for perfection, so he could never find the genre in which to express himself"(p.8).

Bloomfield's suggestion that the Piers genre could be appropriately called "apocalpse" is outside of our frame of reference. More to our point is Bloomfield's discernment of three literary types forming the bases for that apocalyptic genre in Piers Ploughman; with some modification, these are the types that form the basis of the development of Israel Potter; 1) The allegorical dream narrative; 2) The Dialogue, Consolatio or debate; 3) The encyclopedic satire. This is as accurate a defining of the purposes and success of Melville in Israel Potter as we are ever likely to achieve. For the work is in every sense a dream narrative; how else does one man meet such a parade of notables, a veritable galaxy of his country's hall of revolutionary heroes? The dialogue or exchange with these heroes and attempts at consolation is the core of the work's ultimate importance. The satire, of the English, of Ben Franklin, of religion, of war, of Israel himself, is encyclopedic. And these three types are woven into one by Melville.

There are basic traditional steps in the consolation poem which are superbly well satisfied by Melville. One medievalist has suggested a codification into four skeletal steps.[1] First, "there will be an opening description of the narrator's spiritual inertia." In this section, the principal character will be described as plagued by illness and harassed, perhaps, by a death wish. "He will probably express a desire for help, but at the same time acknowledge that he knows where to find it." Thus we find in Pearl the narrator grieving for his lost jewel at the place where it fell from him:

> Before that spot my hands I wrung
> For the carefull cold that seized on me;
> A wicked grief lodged in my heart
> Though understanding would have brought me peace.
> I mourned my pearl which there was locked
> With violence with swiftly reasonings fought,
> Though the nature of Christ would have
>   taught me comfort.[2]

So, too, do we find in Israel Potter the young man distraught after the loss of his love, occasioned by the intransigency of the parents involved. "Like the leaflets of that evergreen, all the

fibres of his heart trembled with him; tears fell from his eyes."
He makes an attempt to resolve his situation by returning home
with money and the promise of a future as a good provider; "but
if hopes of his sweetheart winged his returning flight, such hopes
were not destined to be crowned with fruition. The dear, false
girl was another's." Israel is burdened by the sense of profound
loss of familial and amorous ties; his career thereafter is a
search for an explanation of this loss and an education in the
capacity of the common man to learn the lessons of attainable
felicities.

The second step in the consolation poem is one in which
"the distracted narrator will perform a positive action which
will precipitate a change of scene, whereupon new characters
will appear who will be projections of different fragments of
himself or his environment." This change of scene is generally
to the country of the mind, but this is not an aspect honored by
Melville, though it will be pointed out how Melville takes pains
to suggest the dream quality of Israel's experience. In any
event, Israel takes that positive step, which is the abandonment
of his acreage to heed the call of the revolutionary army. In so
doing, he asserts the patriotic self-denial that elevates him to
the embodiment of his country's mass society; he is as ill-equip-
ped as that mass society; his problems of identity, of the true
significance of life, liberty and the pursuit of happiness are
theirs. The new characters he encounters are indeed "projections of different fragments of himself." Franklin, Jones and
Allen are all Americans and as such are part of Israel's com-
posite experience, but they all have contrasting ideas of the
American experiment and different solutions to Israel's and
America's problems.

The third step is merely an extension of the second,
where "the argument of the poem will be conducted through dialogue between narrator and the new characters. This is the
most elastic part of the genre." Indeed it is. In Pearl, there
is only one new character introduced, the mysterious lady a-
cross the river, with whom the narrator argues and becomes
enlightened as to the true nature of his loss and the pointlessness
of his mourning. For Amans in Confessio Amantis, it is fortun-
ate for him that he encounters Venus who, after questioning
him, sends him Genius for a guide and confessor. It is necessary
for the grieving person to bare his soul to those who will help
him, although this is not the same as the highly structured for-

mal confession by which Gower, in a masterstroke, brings a new unity to his modification of the entire genre. There is this constant baring of the soul in Israel Potter, a seeking after sympathy and education, a notion that if all is told all will be explained and consolation will be forthcoming. This is by no means the same device as that employed by Gower, for it affords Melville little opportunity for extending his dramatic or narrative freedom. He had no need of further license. The use of the frequent confessions of Israel underscore the object of his wanderings, which is the solution of his psychological and political and moral malaises. Israel bares his soul continually in the fond hope that this will lead to education and to communication and a deepening of the bonds with his fellow man. Thus he tells it all in Chapter Four to Sir John Millet, in an almost compulsive act, before it is at all certain that his number is up. In Chapter Five, he conceals nothing in the brief interview with King George. In Chapter Six, he reveals his story, aided by two glasses of Perry and some cold beef, to Horne Tooke, James Bridges and John Woodcock. In Chapter Seven, Franklin evinces an interest in Potter's adventures; "Israel immediately began, and related to the Doctor all his adventures to the present time.." In Chapter Fourteen, Jones commands the "yellow lion," as he calls Israel, to "plump on the woolsack. . . and spin the yarn." Israel does not hesitate. Israel never talks to Ethan Allen, but this is Melville's surest touch of irony. In fact, Israel makes no comment at all on the character or behaviour of Allen; he does not quite know what to make of the performance and does not recognise what Melville skillfully suggests: that Allen is the true guide and unimpeachable man and American. Israel has the solution under his nose but never quite sees it; he pushes on in his journey through life. But there is a dialogue between Israel and all the other characters, not always explicitly on his problems, but always inferential to the issues which confront him. Even with Ethan Allen, there is an interplay between the two men, a dialogue by example; it is insufficient in that Israel does not understand what Allen is trying to tell him and all the world by his example.

In the fourth step in the consolation poem the interaction between the afflicted persons and those to whom he turns for help will conclude " with a tense moment in which the disturbed person will waver, then achieve a final revelation which will bring about his return, usually to home. "This return to home is not always intended as a physical transportation, though in the case of Israel it is precisely that. It is also more, provided that we see Israel, at the end of the novel and his journey, as learning something fundamental about his own personal nature and that of his countrymen and country. One guide to this might very well lie with the de-secularising that Melville imposes upon the end of Potter's original narrative. While the old veteran builds the end of his story on the unfairness of the law and the questionable ethics of his brothers in disposing of Israel's share of the family fortune, it is stressed that this is not Melville's concern. Melville takes care of these details, which he regards as almost extraneous and which must be regarded as such if we are to avoid the pettiness that mars the Life and Remarkable Adventures, in a few short lines:

> Best followed now is this life, by hurry-
> ing like itself, to a close.
> Few things remain.
> He was repulsed in efforts after a pension
> by certain caprices of the law.
> His scars proved his only medals.
> He dictated a little book, the record of his
> fortunes (Ch. XXVI).

These are unimportant in Melville; they were vital in the original story because Potter had gained nothing else from his journeys, had achieved no revelation concerning his life experience and had retained his original concern with material aspects. Confronted with the remnants of the old family home, Melville's Israel, "blindly ranging to and fro," is aware that there is something to be learnt from this collapse. Though Melville does not overtly inform us of this, it is apparent that this is a culminatory experience and that the various highways and byways which took Israel to the sides of great and small men, through sickness and deprivation, have all finally converged. If he did not know exactly what to make of the magnificent defiance of Ethan Allen, and if he was not quite sure what had been wrong with the philosophy of life expounded variously by John Paul Jones and Benjamin Franklin, there is one short moment of revelation when he traces his total misfortune in the dust of the old home:

> " 'Father!' Here, "raking with his staff,
> "my father would sit, and here, my
> mother, and here I, little infant, would

totter between, even as now, once again, on the very same spot, but in the unroofed air, I do. The ends meet. Plough away, friend " (Ch. XXVI).

The ends have met and life has gone its full circle. There are those who guess the pattern very early and gear themselves for the dizzy turns. There are those who catch the design mid-way through life, like Dante and his fateful encounter with the Leopard, and who thereafter have some idea of the significance of life. Israel finds the pattern only after the whole circle has been described and his life is at its end. But Melville has not allowed him to die without that last revelation.

Finding absolute models for the kind of progession structured by Melville in Israel Potter is without any real reward; it should not be suggested for a moment that Melville had Gower's Confessio Amantis or Boethius' Consolation of Philosophy specifically in mind when he set out to rework the original adventure. It is essential that we see the parallels between Israel Potter and the medieval quest allegory because without them we lose the sense of structure and purpose in the wandering of Potter and finally have no idea of progression on his part towards a greater understanding of significant issues; the work remains formless, the incidents are of superficial interest and little sense of religious, political or individual illumination occurs to us. Nor do we have to go back to the Middle Ages to trace possible counterparts of such a progression. The most popular allegory in the language was derived from these sources, was written in the seventeenth century and was admired, imitated and even parodied in Melville's own day: Bunyan's Pilgrim's Progress. Pierre is difficult to see as "a Pilgrim's Progress in reverse," as someone suggested;[3] but Israel Potter is profitably entertained as Melville's secular charting of the course of Bunyan's allegory, modified by borrowing from other, more tractable, allegorical examples. Melville was not alone. Macaulay observed, "The attempts which have been made to improve and to imitate The Pilgrim's Progress are not to be numbered. It has been done into verse; it has been done into modern English.... But the peculiar glory of Bunyan is that those who hated his doctrines have tried to borrow the help of his genius."[4]

It is the peculiar glory of Melville that he eschewed parody of Pilgrim's Progress, unlike Hawthorne in his "Celestial

Railroad." He had no part in imitation as William R. Weeks did in The Pilgrim's Progress in the Nineteenth Century, with its final edition published in the same year in which Melville acquired the Life and Remarkable Adventures, 1849; nor does Melville find himself in the same company as the author of the anonymous Pilgrim's Progress in the Last Days, printed in 1843, or with James Benton, whose The California Pilgrim was published in Sacramento in 1853, the year before Melville finally got around to writing Israel Potter. These works by Benton, Weeks, the unknown Bunyanian and Hawthorne himself are interesting to varying degrees as commentaries on Melville's work. Melville could not have been particularly excited by Weeks' counterpart to Bunyan's Christian, his pro-Calvinist Thoughtful, and his sweeping indictment of such ungodly activities as theater-going, drinking alcoholic beverages and breaking of the Sabbath. But he would have been in accord with the anti-slavery impulses of Weeks, and might have found something to admire in Weeks' dislike of "Perfectionists, Unionists, Campbellites, Millerites, Annihilators, Universalists, Mormons, Transcendentalists, Swedenborgians, Fourierrites" and all those whose perfect plans for salvation of the species appear to question the efficacy of the old religion.[5] Pilgrim's Progress in the Last Days expands the scope of attack beyond the theological anti-liberalism in Weeks and "successfully allegorizes certain conventional objects of attack less successfully treated in . . . other works, including transcendentalism, classical humanism, and progress as reflected in a contemporary faith in modern science and invention."[6] From Ben Franklin's silly plans for a better shoe heel and shuttle-cock to the dehumanizing industrial scene of brickmaking, Melville snipes and strikes at invention and science wherever both threaten to subvert their relationship with man and become master of the humanity they are supposed to serve.

Benton's The California Pilgrim is perhaps the most specifically American of all. In it, the pilgrim sets out to find the Celestial City in the west, in California. The Eastern part of the country is beyond redemption; the pilgrim's home city of Doomsend has been consumed by a fiery deluge, and he leaves to travel through the wilderness towards the golden west, where hope abides for the American people. In fact, evil has already corrupted San Francisco and Sacramento, but there is the suggestion that, after a cleansing fire, California will assume the apocalytical proportions of the New Jerusalem, which will be situated in the western wilderness of the United States. This is part of the mythos of the virgin land which sought to establish the detergent qualities of the west when that untrammeled part of the American cosmography is brought to bear on the American character. Henry Nash Smith noted that this western wilderness beyond the Ohio frontier had an exhilarating influence on Melville, and that although he never devoted whole works to the theme of the vital wildness of the west, and that while Melville very often showed no special sensitivity to the west beyond that of the cultivated cultural primitivist, he was capable of incorporating and personally extending the western mythos through modification into his private vision.[7] Smith found significant Melville's corralling of two images of the White Steed of the Prairies and the Vermont colt terrified by the proximity of a buffalo robe, in Chapter XLII of Moby Dick, " The Whiteness of the Whale." Combined in these two images are "the sinister blend of majesty and terror" together with "the paradisiacal innocence of the Wild West."[8] When the character of Ethan Allen is discussed it will be shown that Melville found in this Vermonter the ideal, quintessential American spirit, that which he hoped would one day permeate all levels of the American society. For although Allen was that Vermont colt by birth, "his spirit was essentially Western" and his whole presence in Melville is obviously built on the same lines of that "magnificent milk-white charger, large-eyed, small-headed, bluff-chested, and with the dignity of a thousand monarchs in his lofty, overscorning carriage. . . . A most imperial and archangelical apparition of that unfallen, western world, which to the eyes of the old trappers and hunters revived the glories of those primeval times when Adam walked majestic as a god, bluff-browed and fearless as this mighty steed " (Ch. XLII). This is precisely the way in which mighty Ethan Allen walks. Melville describes him as "frank, bluff, . . . hearty as a harvest;" "Though born in New England, he exhibited no trace of her character" (Ch. XXII). All of the best qualities of that European stock had gone into the making of this new man of America, and this new man of America wanted no part of the East. The East could serve Franklin and be a good place for the aquatic John Paul Jones occasionally to come ashore from his piratical acts; for the man of true quality, it had nothing to offer.

      For Melville's New Jerusalem in Israel Potter, the Celestial City for which Israel sets out in search after rejecting and being rejected by the land of his birth, is nowhere to be found. What those who had drawn up progresses based on the arrival in some New Jerusalem had elected to ignore was that in certain ways this was another form of meliorism, another plan for salvation that was sure to work if only rigidly followed, and Melville was not taking part in this old apocalyptical liberalism. Melville is interested in what he felt to be the possible, not the visionary, and he was sure he had found in Ethan Allen the type of the new American whose spirit, infectious enough, could transform the nation away from the materialism cloaked in meticulousness on one hand and the predatory selfishness on the other. There is no New Jerusalem, though Allen qualifies as a citizen. Like the kingdom of God, which is supposed to be within the believer, the New Jerusalem is also within the man even as he walks about in a tarnished world that deserves to be destroyed. Allen has achieved the status of a citizen of the New Jerusalem, but in it the modus vivendi predicates continual struggle. Israel is seeking a cure-all for his ills and he hopes to pass through the gates into a state of permanent quietude; his activities fleeing from soldiers and fighting with the Bon Homme Richard strengthen this desire to come to some honorable halt. It is part of the reason why he does not have anything to say about Allen that he finds incomprehensible the message that Allen is Allen agonistes, a temper of mind and body capable of survival in the west where he belongs. It is, moreover, a temper that has little to do with military heroics or physical violence, for herein John Paul Jones is most accomplished in the novel. It has to do with a recognition of life as struggle from beginning to end; it is the determination never to abdicate the responsibilities of each individual in such a struggle; these responsibilities are consistently to fellow fighters and spring from a recognition of a common brotherhood and a common enemy. Ethan, in fighting against the British, is fighting for them in that he is struggling for all men against the vices of tyranny and oppression. Jones is fighting for himself, and Franklin is fighting not at all; subterfuge is the latter's method. His reward, if it ever comes, will be beyond. Allen alone has achieved.

    Though it is not my purpose to find a high degree of relationship between Israel Potter and any formal allegory of renown, including Pilgrim's Progress, it is urged that the picture of London drawn in the chapter entitled "In the City of Dis" represents Melville's rendering of Isaiah's and Bunyan's City of Destruction, which Israel has mistakenly been approaching ever since he set out from the land of his fathers in search of the Celestial City.[9] Melville was summarising urban horrors in his picture of London, and he could have easily done the same with Israel's visit to Paris on behalf of the Revolutionary cause: he did not do so, however, because for the real Israel Potter London and no other city had represented his greatest hopes. The real Potter had become disillusioned with the great city, but had clung to it for decades as if he expected salvation to come and change it in the way Benton anticipated a New Jerusalem to emerge out of the decadent cities of the West coast of the United States. Melville's Potter was to the end never quite sure of the evil that lurked in the city; its initial impact on him so stunned him that he never recovered until that moment when he finally left London bound for home. As for his astonishment at London, which he had envisioned as a Celestial City, the New Jerusalem on earth where he would find peace and prosperity, "for forty years he never recovered from that surprise--never, till dead, had done with his wondering" (Ch. XXIV).

For London was the exact opposite of Bunyan's Celestial City, and Melville dwelled on those differences. Christian looks through the open gates where those accepted are entering,

> and behold, the City shone like the sun, the Streets also were paved with Gold, and in them walked many men, with Crowns on their heads, palms in their hands, and golden harps to sing praises withall.[10]

To get there, of course, Christian and all others who hope to enter must die;

> Now I further saw, that betwixt them and the Gate was a River, but there was no Bridge to go over; the River was very deep; at the sight therefore of this River, the Pilgrims were much stounded, but the men that went with them, said, You must go through, or you cannot come at the Gate.[11]

And though terrified at the prospect of death and wavering to the end, Christian does die:

> And with that, a great darkness and horror fell upon Christian, so that he could not see before him; also here he in great measure lost his senses, so that he could neither remember nor orderly talk of any of those sweet refreshments that he had met with in the way of his Pilgrimage.[12]

Almost all of Chapter XXIV concerns itself not with the city of London as with that bridge across the river; commentators sometimes seem to place the brickmaking scene in London; Melville says quite clearly that it is "some ten or fifteen miles" from London. So Melville's concern is with the passage across the river to the materialistic Celestial City, the City of Destruction. There is no mistaking that he intends all those who enter that city first to die, as in Bunyan:

> Hung in long, sepulchral arches of stone, the black, besmoked bridge seemed a huge scarf of crape, festooning the river across. Similar funeral festoons spanned it to the west, while westward, towards the sea, tiers and tiers of jetty colliers lay moored, side by side, fleets of black swans.
> The Thames, . . . polluted by continual vicinity to man, . . . created and hissed, then shot balefully through the Erebus arches, desperate as the lost souls of the harlots, who, every night, took the same plunge. Meantime, here and there, like awaiting hearses, the coal-scows drifted along, poled broadside, pell-mell to the current (Ch. XXIV).

All is funereal, and Israel, like Christian, is befuddled by the sense of death. The "gulf-stream of humanity" flows over the bridge of death and into the city, "uninvoked ghosts in Hades." "Some of the wayfarers wore a less serious look; some seemed hysterically merry; but the mournful faces had an earnestness not seen in the others; because man, 'poor player', succeeds better in life's tragedy than comedy." Just as darkness and horror fall upon Christian at the moment of death, so, for Israel, "as in eclipses, the sun was hidden; the air darkened; the whole dull, dismayed aspect of things . . . ." It is the correct light in which to view London and any other conglomeration of vices assembled under the urban aegis; Melville sees the city about to be destroyed by fire and brimstone, as the City of Destruction was destroyed: "as if some neighbouring volcano, belching its premonitory smoke, were about to whelm the great town, as Herculaneum and Pompeii, or the Cities of the Plain."

Israel enters the City of Destruction and it is not consumed by fire; instead, it is as if the city consumes Israel into its intestines and concealed him there for forty years. Melville's three Armageddons both "slay and secrete their victims." If his confrontation with the city has taught him anything, it has put into his mind suspicions that unhappiness is the constant companion of all humanity. He does not learn of any alternative to unhappiness, but he glimpses one fundamental truth of life, probably for the first time. Traversing the bridge of death from the Surrey to the Middlesex side, "Israel's heart was prophetically heavy; foreknowing, that being of this race, felicity could never be his lot." And still Israel does not give up. His wandering in the city of Dis is almost a penetential act, but it is never accompanied by despair. Just as those "stoic impulses" are at work, so does Israel hold on to his sense of sanity

> as those tough old oaks of the cliffs, which, though hacked at by hail-stones of tempests, and even wantonly maimed by the passing woodman, still, however cramped by rival trees and fettered by rocks, succeed, against all odds, in keeping the vital nerve of the taproot alive (Ch. XXV).

This refusal to go under is the single but redeeming grace of Israel Potter. It begins as faith in himself, as he cuts away from the family to make his fortune and hopefully to win his girl. It expands into love of country as he goes to fight at Bunker Hill, and sustains him through the seduction attempts of Sir John and the King. The lures of Franklin and John Paul Jones are infinitely more subtle, but Israel survives both encounters; by the time he comes to the bridge of death leading into the City of Destruction this piece of steel has been tempered beyond either self-interest or patriotism into something so fundamental that Israel himself is at pains to identify it; yet it prevents him from dropping out of the race; he remains a man and is capable of dreams, even though those dreams are at times harassing hullucination akin to the dreams of the demented. But for all his forty years of wandering in the City of Dis, Israel is still able to preserve himself for the journey back home and his ultimate education.

Who is Israel Potter that he sould have such resilience? Is he Bunyan's Ignorance, the "very brisk lad" from out of the country of Conceit, who meets Christian after walking down "a little crooked Lane"? Christian warns Ignorance that his journey to the Celestial City might be all in vain, because "thou camest not in at the Wicket-gate, that is, at the head of this way: thou camest in hither through that same crooked lane...." But Ignorance is bull-headed: "Gentlemen, ye be utter strangers to me, I know you not, be content to follow the Religion of your Countrey, and I will follow the religion of mine. I hope all will be well."[13] He trusts completely in the dictates of his heart and in good thoughts and good deeds. In vain does Christian explain that Ignorance can be saved only through complete faith in God and not by his deeds. Ignorance suffers a fate not unlike that of Israel when the latter applies for a pension. At the gates of the Celestial City, he cannot produce the required certificate and is dispatched into Hell.

It has been suggested that Ignorance, " the disingenuous pilgrim trapped in an ambiguous world midway between the forsaken City of Destruction and the sought-after Celestial City," stands at the center of Nathaniel Hawthorne's art,[14] traceable in such figures as the narrator of the obvious "Celestial Railroad," in Dimmesdale, the young hero of "My Kinsman, Major Molineux" and others, who exist in the counterpart to Bunyan's "wilderness of this world, " which is "a trackless American forest of puritanical pine trees."[15] Certainly there are strong elements of Ignorance in Israel's character; they both share an uninformed obduracy, both seem attracted to the crooked little lanes of life. Yet it is too limiting to Melville's design to find only Ignorance in the character that is Israel. We must take into account also the quite deliberate manner in which Melville makes Israel into a Christ-figure, no matter how exasperated we may have become at Melville's love of the Christ motif.

A Christ-figure he undoubtedly becomes. When Melville writes in his last chapter, "Requiescat in Pace, " that at Bunker Hill Israel "had received that slit upon the chest, which afterwards, in the affair with the Serapis, being traversed by a cutlass wound, made him now the bescarred bearer of a cross," it does not come completely unexpected. Although the bearer of a cross can easily be an ass, which is not far from patient long-suffering Israel, and is present in Melville in the Encantadas, (where it apparently brought tears to the eyes of James Russell Lowell):[16] "the last seen of lone Hunilla she was passing into Payta town, riding upon a small gray ass; and before her on the ass's shoulders, she eyed the jointed workings of the beast's armorial cross " (Sketch Eight). In Melville's staging of Israel's entry into what he mistakenly imagines to be the New Jerusalem, we have the impression that Christ's Palm Sunday entry into Jerusalem, as King of the Jews, is being echoed; Israel has " several blood-blisters in his palms " and he enters the city, "like the king, from Windsor" (Ch. XXIV). Israel's incarceration in the cell in Squire Woodcock's home and his resurrection after three days in the cell also provoke ideas of Christian symbolism. Melville calls it a "three days' mystery," and he has reinforced the idea of Christian ritual by reminding us of the religious origins of the cell and the Squire's house, which "once formed portion of a religious retreat belonging to the Templars " (Ch. XII). It is not an enjoyable experience, and Israel slowly sinks into a state near to despair: "He mutely raved in the darkness. The delirious sense of the absence of light was soon added to his other delirium as to the contraction of space .... Then he thought the air itself was getting unbearable" (Ch. XII). But that fine, final thread of steel in Israel pulls him through again. The morning of the fourth day comes. "Soon his dumb ravings entirely left him, and gradually, with a sane, calm mind, he revolved all the circumstances of his condition"(Ch. XII).

There is obviously as much parody as serious symbolism in this figuring of Israel as Christ in the cell at Squire Woodcock's home. The cumulative impression at the book's end is that Israel has attained some level of religious merit by his steadfast refusal to fall into despair. If he is like Bunyan's Ignorance in that both, at the end of their lives, are refused a reward because they do not have "certificates," it must be understood that, to Melville, Israel's failure to receive his pension is not very significant and it is treated as such. To the real Israel Potter, it was everything, including the cause of his turn to authorship in his old age. But for Melville the reward of life did not consist of pensions, and Israel is only partly Ignorance; the two are closer in matters of style than in articles of faith. There is much more of Bunyan's Hopeful in Israel Potter. Hopeful is prophetically with Christian when he meets Ignorance briskly stepping out of the crooked lane into the highway of Life. Hopeful is a new convert to Christian's side, "(being made so by the beholding of Christian and Faithful in their words and behaviour, in their sufferings at the fair) who joyned himself unto him, and entering into a brotherly covenant, told him that he would be his Companion."[16] Hopeful is hardly perfect; he has consistently to be educated by Christian, who is his guide and mentor. Yet as they cross the river of death into the Celestial City, it is Hopeful who has the kind of steel that Israel shows:

> Christian began to sink, and crying out to his good friend Hopeful; he said, I sink in deep Waters, the Billows go over my head, all his Waves go over me, Selah.
> Then said the other, Be of good chear, my brother, I feel the bottom, and it is good.[17]

Christian is harassed by apparitions of hobgoblins and evil spirits; it is Hopeful who keeps his head above water time and again, comforting him and raising his spirits

> saying, Brother, I see the Gate, and men standing by it to receive us. But Christian would answer, 'Tis you, 'tis you they wait for, you have been Hopeful ever since I knew you; and so have you, said he to Christian.[18]

Christian wavers in his faith and wonders aloud whether he has been right in his belief, and whether God has not in fact forsaken him:

> Then said Hopeful, My Brother, you have quite forgot the Text, where its said of the wicked, <u>There is no band in their death, but their strength is firm, they are not troubled as other men, neither are they plagued like other men.</u> These troubles and distresses that you go through in these Waters, are no sign that God hath forsaken you, but are sent to try you, whether you will call to mind that which

heretofore you have received of his goodness, and live upon him in your distresses.[19]

This is fundamental Christian theology and perhaps will appear too orthodox to be attributed to Melville. In a sense, it is; Melville's modifications give it a new reality, and those modifications adapt Hopeful's theological roots to a more secular soil. Bunyan was writing classic allegory; Melville was not. The important conclusion bypasses theological speculation to see Israel Potter as a quietly optative work, reconciliatory and spiritually progressive; it deals with possibilities and "attainable felicities" and is not concerned with formal religious solutions. The lesson that Hopeful preaches Melville adapts as an instruction to the artist: "For just as extreme suffering, without hope, is intolerable to the victim, so, to others, is its depiction without some corresponding delusive mitigation" (Ch. XXV). But it is also adapted as the prevailing philosophy of Israel Potter; the two worthy characters Potter and Allen are those who suffer most and, by their example, teach others the invincible strength of the determined soul in the assaulted body.

This is the same lesson taught by Melville in depicting the character of Hunilla; she is blessed because she never gives up. She has her religious alliances, "the strong persuasions of her Romish faith"; but it is something else, that center of steel fashioned out of hope, that prevents her from despairing. Genial old Jimmy Rose is made of the same stuff, though his style is more urbane. Reduced to penury, he was quite content to "crawl through life, and peep about among the marbles and mahoganies for contumelious tea and toast"; he loses neither the courtliness of his manners nor the bloom of his rose-red cheeks. Why? "Perhaps at bottom Jimmy was too thoroughly good and kind to be made from any cause a man-hater. And doubtless it at last seemed irreligious to Jimmy even to shun mankind." This, together with the spirit of Israel Potter, Hunilla and others who dare to affirm the necessity of love, was the testament of Melville even as he appeared in his own life to be adopting the very same morose privacy that Jimmy spurns. When Maria Melville hoped for a situation where Herman would be "compelled to more intercourse with his fellow creatures," she was witnessing not a surrender but a continuous struggle. Melville knew what the alternative was; if it seemed irreligious to Jimmy Rose ever to shun mankind, Bartleby failed to see the heresy he was exemplifying in turning his back on mankind. When he dies and at last reposes with kings and counsellors, he has attained a state of delusive permanence. Melville saw a mutual responsibility between mankind and the individual as the ideal condition of life; Bartleby makes the tragic mistake of seeing it as the only possible condition; when mankind betrays him, as he feels it has done, he regards himself as free from any responsibility to contribute to the world. Israel acts as if to question mankind, even in cruel times, is akin to questioning God. Vicissitudes showered upon him weaken his social and financial position, but are never allowed to sever the bonds that tie individual to community. This was the core of Melville's "ruthless democracy." It elevated the mass of humanity to a position far exceeding that of the sum of its parts. It was the one consistent religion that Melville ever had. "Bartleby the Scrivener" is not of necessity a wavering in faith; it is as much a literary exercise in the depiction of the greatest of all heresies in the religion that Melville followed.

Chapter Five

Harpoon into Plowshare

Melville's abandonment of the heroic vehicle for metaphysical questioning after he had reached its epitome in Moby Dick demanded a major shift in symbolic emphasis. Ahab's last words, "Thus, I give up the spear," signals this shift. Pierre represents Melville's failure to effect this transition smoothly; it was too hurriedly written. In Israel Potter Melville makes that transition. If Ahab and Melville are giving up the spear after exhausting its potential and discovering its destructive power, what is the alternative instrument by which life is to be led? As a profound reader of the Bible, Melville must have known the answer for a long time; the homiletic aspects of Israel Potter, and the major symbolic shift in Melville, take as their textual source the words of Isaiah as he prophesies the coming of the Kingdom of Peace:

> And they shall beat their swords into plowshares,
> And their spears into pruning hooks;
> Nation shall not lift up sword against nation,
> Neither shall they learn war any more.
> (Isaiah 2:4)

This is in the kindom to come, the optimum human condition, requiring the cleansing by fire. The islands called Encantadas have been desolated in precisely such a manner. Thus Jeremiah quotes the Lord as promising to punish the house of Israel for its many transgressions, "to make their land desolate, and a perpetual hissing" (18:16), and promises again later in that same parable of the Potter and the broken vessel that he "will make this city desolate, and a hissing" (19:8). In the Encantadas, published just before Israel Potter, Melville tells us that on those islands, "No voice, no low, no howl is heard; the chief sound of life here is a hiss" (Sketch 1). The Potter, in Jeremiah's story, breaks the vessel of clay in order to build a better work; so will God destroy the house of Israel in order to build a better world. So is Israel Potter almost broken on the wheel of the world before he learns his lesson.

Isaiah prophesies a turn from the spear to the p l o w and in Israel Potter we have this shift from the harpoon to the p l o w. The p l o w is the dominant symbol in Israel Potter, a positive religious correlate, opposite to the harpoon in Moby Dick, which is baptized in nomine diaboli after it has been made of twelve apostolic strands. Concomitant with the plow is the earth. Antithetical to the plow and the tilled earth is the spear, which John Paul Jones intransigently grasps and which almost seduces Potter, and the brick or burnt earth, which is the abomination of the soil and, again, which almost seduces Israel completely. The city is a conglomerate of burnt earth, of the hideous industrial process. Its corruption springs naturally from this perversion of the natural process; the alienation that is evident in the faces passing Israel as he watches the world go by on London bridge is retributory from this sin of subversion of the basic order. The plow and the good earth, the spear and the burnt earth, these are the antithetical symbols that give unity and significance to the story, Israel Potter. Israel himself should have his home in the good soil, but flees in search of delusion, Celestial Cities which do not exist. As he leaves home the fibres of his heart tremble "like the leaflets of that evergreen" (Ch. II); so in London he is a tough old oak "keeping the vital nerve of the tap-root alive" (Ch. XXV); so, home at last in the soil where he was born, "he died the same day that the oldest oak on his native hills was blown down" (Ch. XXVI).

All of this is prefigured in that marvellous first chapter of Israel Potter, which he penned without recourse to the Life and Remarkable Adventures, then turned aside to follow the old man's story until the point arrived where he would return to his own imagination; even in those first chapters Melville draws threads from the fabric of the first chapter for the new pattern the story of Israel Potter was taking.

That first chapter has been recognized by several critics as invaluable to the understanding of Israel Potter. In one story, the description of Israel's place of birth dwells on images of light and dark, of space and confinement and of solitude and danger that prefigure the later obscuring of the satiric passages, reappearing again mid-way in the novel with Israel's symbolic entombment and finally, with great impact, in the brickyard scene at the close of the novel, "the suggestions of solitude, immurement and confinement, and of darkness and danger," expressed or latent in the first chapter, are now developed.[1] Another study, which sees the novel as representing the "metamorphosis of Superman" and a demonstration by Melville of the triumph of the common man, finds proof in this first chapter of the deliberate elevation of Israel to the level of superman able to mix with the other major characters, who are themselves all built on the Titanic scale. "The mixing of the superman and the common man results in a metamorphosis of the former into the latter. By the end of the book the superman of the beginning has disappeared and been replaced by the common man."[2]

Israel discovers at the very close of the book and near the close of his life that "the ends meet." Coming back to the land of his birth, and the very fields in which he first roamed, for the first time he realizes that the goal, the New Jerusalem, which he has pursued so assiduously from the day he determined to leave his father's house, was right there in those same fields where he was born. That New Jerusalem is for each individual man to rebuild out of the mistakes of his own life; it is certainly not to be found in the materialism of the city of London or of Paris. The country that Melville describes as having been the birthplace of Israel symbolises the terrestrial environment that surrounds each individual who wishes to progress towards a more salubrious expression of life. In the New Jerusalem of Melville and Israel, there is no luxury, no attendant angels or heavenly music, none of the celestial sloth that depictors of God's kingdom seem too often to favor. In that "high land" where the first settlers dwelled, only hard work brings reward.

The book opens with Melville's proposition that a traveller in these parts will find "ample food for poetic reflection in the singular scenery of a country, which, owing to the ruggedness of the soil and its lying out of the track of all public conveyances, remain almost as unknown to the general tourist as the interior of Bohemia" (Ch. 1). We have described here both the allegorical traveller in quest of something ultimately more rewarding and Melville's first sketches of the countryside of the real life. The traveller must go on foot, "in the good old Asiatic style," as Christian does, "neither rushed along by a locomotive" in the fashion of Hawthorne's life-travellers in the "Celestial Railroad," or using even a stagecoach. The soil is rugged and the journey is hard; for these reasons, few travel there.

It is a travel through high ground. "For nearly the whole of the distance, you have the continual sensation of being upon some terrace in the moon. The feeling of the plain or the valley is never yours; scarcely the feeling of the earth"(Ch. 1). Far below the traveller, "mapped out in its beauty, the valley of the Housatonic lies endlessly along at your feet . . . . You seem to be Bootes driving in heaven." This is as the Kingdom of Peace is described in Isaiah, where "the mountain of the Lord's house shall be established in the top of the mountains, And shall be exalted above the hills" (2:2). In the bucolic reality of these mountains the principal inhabitants are horses, cattle and sheep and an occasional charcoal-burner or maple sugar-boiler. These are the occupations of the poor, for this is the land of the poor in spirit; a little farming is done, but "no man by that means accumulates a fortune from this thin and rocky soil." The high land is soon deserted by most people for the lower regions; the first provides spartan safety, a kind of moral excellence, which is soon abandoned in favor of the pursuit of riches, although those who dwell there are subject to "the unwholesome miasmas generated by breaking into the rich valleys and alluvial bottoms of primeval regions." The signs of ancient industry are about; here the symbol is the block of stone, as in London it is the brick of burnt earth. The early settlers knew the value of labor; Melville wonders that they "should have taken such wonderful pains to enclose so ungrateful a soil; that they should have accomplished such herculean undertakings with so light prospect of rewards."

Just as this New Jerusalem described by Melville promises a life of hard work as its daily reward, so also is it susceptible to the seasons. It is, of course, the mirror of man's own life. Melville takes us through the seasons: "In fine clear June days, the bloom of these mountains is beyond expression delightful. Last visiting these heights ere she vanishes, Spring, like the sunset, flings her sweetest charms upon them." Flowers bloom and birds sing; moreover, it is the moment of religious celebration. The twin summits of Saddleback form "the two-steepled natural cathedral of Berkshire." There are eagles and hawks a-preying, but there are also yellow-birds and robins in the flowers. Melville elsewhere had portrayed these birds as capacities of the soul, and the mountains as symbols of spiritual elevation as he does in Israel Potter. In the "Tryworks" chapter of Moby Dick: "And there is a Catskill eagle in some souls that can alike dive down into the blackest gorges, and soar out of them again and become invisible in sunny spaces. And even if he for ever flies within the gorge, the gorge is in the mountains; so that even in his lowest swoop the mountain eagle is still higher than other birds upon the plain, even though they soar" (Moby Dick, Chap. XCVII). The different birds, the mountains and the gorges have a similar religious connotation in that first chapter of Israel Potter: "Meanwhile the air is vocal with their hymns, and your own soul joys in the general joy . . . . You cannot help singing yourself when all around you raise such hosannas."

In the autumn of life comes the time of intimations of mortality. " The traveller is beset, at perilous turns, by dense masses of fog." He must lead his horse "down some scowling glen, where the road steeply dips among grim rocks, only to rise as abruptly again." There are ghost-like objects in the haze that, closely examined, tell tales of death and disaster. And "in winter this region is blocked with snow. Inaccessible and impassable, those wild, unfrequented roads, which in August are overgrown with high grass, in December are drifted to the arm-pit with the white fleece from the sky." This is the country of Israel's birth, to which he returns at life's end. "How could he ever have dreamed, when involved in the autumnal vapors of these mountains, that worse bewilderments awaited him three thousands miles across the sea, wandering forlorn in the coal-fog of London."

It is in this high land that Israel should have spent his life. He had had his fling in the wide world after first leaving home, as hunter and harpooner and trader, as Melville had had his fling away from home in his youth. He knows his duty; when he has been finally rejected by his girl, "stifling his pain, he chose rather to plough than be ploughed. Farming weans man from his sorrows. That tranquil pursuit tolerates nothing but tranquil meditations. There, too, in mother earth, you may plant and reap; not, as in other things, plant and see the planting torn up by the roots" (Ch. III). When at last he leaves the fields behind him, it is not his fault, really; he goes to fight the British, one incident leads to another, and soon he is on English soil. There is no blame attached to Israel for leaving the land; it is his ignorant wandering thereafter that needs to be questioned. It should be clear that when Melville used the p l o w symbolically in Israel Potter it has little to do with an agricultural pursuit, except as a harmonising of the symbolic setting; it is concerned with the patient life of dedication to honest work, whether it be the toils of the worker in the fields or the writer in his study. Orare est labore. What Ben Franklin represents is not work but exploitation. In the novel itself, the plow is Israel's natural tool, as the pen is Melville's. That first chapter spreads the earth before us and before Israel as a challenge to duty, which Israel passes by.

Israel is soon in his life a patriot and ultimately a steadfast soul; he is also human. Like Ignorance in Bunyan, he seeks the crooked little paths. He learns little dishonesties; the real Potter described in the Life and Remarkable Adventures how he had become "adept at deception."[3] Melville develops this weakness in Israel's character through the subtlest use of the "Clothes Philosophy" outside of The Confidence Man; it is interesting to compare, in this respect, the modus operandi of Israel and the Confidence Man. Both are Christ figures in a hostile world and both resort to dissimulation, subterfuge and disguise in order to face the world and achieve their aims. The Confidence Man wears no more than eight disguises; Israel Potter, often with no real provocation, puts on different and deceptive clothing at least as often; it is a display that Melville added to the Life and Remarkable Adventures, to reveal something new about the character he was recreating.

Melville's use of the clothes philosophy in Israel Potter goes beyond mere disguise. As Israel rushes from the field of the farmer to that of the soldier at Bunker Hill, Melville reminds us that "while we revel in broadcloth, let us not forget what we owe to linsey-woolsey" (Ch. II). In the same chapter he exchanges clothes with an old man: "Israel looked suddenly metamorphosed from youth to old age; just like a man of eighty he looked." It is a coat of all colors, patchworked. His clothes betray him; his British navy shirt, which he has kept, causes him to be captured (Ch. IV). After escaping, he tears off the offending collar, then is befriended by Sir John Millet and wears his clothes: "Israel cheered up, and in the course of two or three weeks had so fattened his flanks, that he was able completely to fill Sir John's old buckskin breeches" (Ch. IV). He is so impressed after King George has spoken to him that Israel "would soon have sported the red coat" (Ch. V). Before meeting Squire Woodcock's pro-American clique, he is disguised in strange clothes by a farmer to facilitate the rendezvous (Ch. VI). To escape from the dead Squire's home, he wears the man's clothes and "felt convinced that he would well pass for Squire Woodcock's genuine phantom" (Ch. XIII). Shortly after this, he exchanges the finery for the old clothes on a scarecrow (Ch. XIII). A few pages later in the same chapter, he buys a new set of clothes from another farmer. Before entering the City of Dis, he is dressed in some "mouldy old rags, . . . clothing not improbably, as he surmised, left there on the bank [of a pond] by some pauper suicide" (Ch. XXII). Another time we learn that his is a "blue-jean career" across which Paul Jones "flits and re-flits like a crimson thread." This is in a chapter entitled "The Shuttle" (Ch. XX).

This is subtle but not masterful work. It seems clear that Israel is being described as a kind of junior confidence-man, an apprentice in the craft with a skill yet to be developed. But this is another instance of Melville's subterranean working in this novel; the touch is all restraint, whereas in Pierre its aim was almost all bravura. So unobtrusive is this working of the clothes philosophy here that it could easily go unnoticed. Melville was prepared for that; where he would have gone for the bold stroke previously, here he puts faith in the accretive process of his art.

But if Israel has both the gentleness of the dove and the wisdom of the serpent, he also has steadfastness enough to keep him uncompromised through his meeting with Sir John and the King. These two represent twin temptations to Israel as he journeys on. Sir John represents a temptation based on Israel's personal familial tragedy. Israel is quickly "charmed by the patriarchal demeanour of this true Abrahamic gentleman," and with a smile on his lips, "and tears of gratitude in his eyes, offered him, from time to time, the plumpest berries of the bed." The King, to whom Israel can be respectful but not subject, offers a more traditional kind of temptation. He is like Bunyan's Demas at the Hill Lucre, who tempts Christian with silver.

As for Israel, "had it not been for our adventurer's disinterested patriotism, he would soon have sported the red coat." Melville explicitly predicts a rich career for Israel, but Israel will not compromise his patriotism, and remains poor but loyal.

At this point Israel has come to mean two intertwined entities; he is an individual human being faced with the miseries most men bear, except in larger quantity; he has come at the same time to represent the mass humanity of his country, America. There are two time scales represented by Melville: historic, and contemporary. The former sees Israel as the young Republic in the days of the Revolution, coming into first contact with the influences and philosophies which all contend in their efforts to gain greatest favor. Secondly, Melville sees Israel as representative of America in the 1850's, at a point where these influences and philosophies have so debilitated the early republican spirit that the state is in gravest danger. Thus, in codifying the characters of Franklin, Jones and Allen, Melville talks at all times in terms of the spirit of America; one appears to be the type of his land, another's savagery seems totally American; these are expressions of Melville's fears concerning the American spirit; he pins his hopes on the third.

On the level of allegory, these three Giants are too complex and too related to the American situation to have any specific counterpart in the English allegorical tradition. Melville underscores the triadic development and epitomises the characters of Franklin, Jones and Allen in a clever stroke towards the close of Chapter XIII, when Israel, with the encounter with Franklin and the incarceration experience behind him, is pressed into naval service and finds himself "a foretopman in his Majesty's ship of the line," Unprincipled, scudding before the wind down channel, in company with the Undaunted, and the Unconquerable. The representation of the major involvement along triadic lines is fairly common; consider Piers Ploughman's search for Do-well, Do-better and Do-best, for example, although we should go no further in comparing Langland's trio to Melville's. There are some exasperating coincidences between the story of Israel Potter, where the plow is the major symbol, and Piers Ploughman: consider that Israel and Piers both receive their call in the fields, whereupon both decide to plow their last "half-acre" before making a move;[4] both have forty or forty-five years of their life simply dismissed by their authors;[5] both quests involve the triadic representation just described; both Piers and Israel become Christ figures, the former being named at one point by Charity, "Piers the Ploughman-- Peter, that is, Christ."[6] Langland, too, strangely utilises the clothes motif, from his initial deliberate dressing of himself in a shepherd's clothing [Prologue] to Christ's appearance in the colors and coat-armor of Piers.[7] And in Melville's novel, when Israel is cornered and questioned on the British battleship after being rejected by every group, he gives his name as "Peter Perkins." (These, of course, are the two other names by which Piers Ploughman is called in Langland's poem.)

In any event, Israel encounters three giants of American history. When he meets the first, Benjamin Franklin, he fully expects help and advice that will return him to the land of his birth. It is with this in mind that he first sets out and then swiftly confesses all to the venerable figure. He gets nothing that is of any use. There is more than a touch of acid in Melville's pen as he sketches the portrait of Franklin. His first appearance, and in contrast to the studied plainness of Potter, is in the garb of a medieval charlatan, an aging mountebank replete with affectation:

> Wrapped in a rich dressing-gown, a fanciful present from an admiring Marchesa, curiously embroidered with algebraic figures like a conjuror's robe, and with a skull-cap of black satin on his hive of a head, the man of gravity was seated at a huge claw-footed old table, round as the zodiac (Ch. VII).

Old age is a dominant impression; the man seems to have "the incredible seniority of an antediluvian." "His white hairs and mild brow spoke of the future as well as the past. He seemed to be seven score years old; that is, three score and ten of prescience added to three score and ten of remembrance, makes just seven score years in all." The room in which he is seated has a "necromantic look,""with cracked walls covered with dust"; Melville has a wicked purpose in all this. Franklin's surroundings and his own appearance bespeak a command of the wisdom of all ages and the books of all countries and all disciplines; he seems to be the sage's sage, totally versatile; yet as soon as he opens his mouth, his didactic and trifling utterances, delivered ex cathedra, fall insipidly on the listener.

What follows is the portrait of a pedantic, parsimonious, mundane and entirely soulless American; full of high sentence and a bit obtuse, he is very much at times the fool. He gives notice that he intends soon to publish a little scientific paper on false heels; he corrects Israel's pronunciation of the name of the river passing through Paris. He drinks no wine with his meal, noting that "plain water is a very good drink for plain men"; he warns Israel against dalliance with the pretty Parisian maid who attends the household, and removes everything from the poor lodger's room not absolutely indispensable for existence. During all this time, Franklin speaks in what is obviously a parody of the substance and style of works such as <u>Poor Richard's Almanac</u>: "if you are poor, avoid wine as a costly luxury; if you are rich, shun it as a fatal indulgence;" "never joke at funerals, or during business transactions; " "an indiscriminate distrust of human nature is the worst consequence of a miserable condition,whether brought about by innocence or guilt." Reading from the <u>Almanac</u>, Israel is driven to exasperation:

>"Oh, confound all this wisdom! It's a sort of insulting to talk wisdom to a man like me. It's wisdom that's cheap, and it's fortune that's dear. That ain't in <u>Poor Richard</u>, but it ought to be," concluded Israel, suddenly slamming down the pamphlet "(Ch. IX).

Thus Melville depicts Ben Franklin.

It is an unfair and unfortunate depiction, unless we recognise the difference between the Franklin dramatically portrayed by Melville and the clarification when, in Chapter Eight, Melville delivers a careful analysis of another Ben Franklin. The difference between the two is the difference between the allegorical and scientific methods. When Melville is dramatising the meeting between Israel and Franklin he is dealing in allegory and is armed with poetic license; when he seeks to clarify that image he has obligations to truth. He admits that in allegorizing the impact of Franklin on the American spirit, he has given an incomplete picture of the man himself, who could hardly have foreseen how succeeding generations would have adapted aspects of his philosophy and ignored others; "the narrator Melville feels more as if he were playing with one of the sage's worsted hose, than reverentially handling the honored hat which once oracularly sat upon his brow " (Ch. VIII). In building the allegorical picture , Melville has deliberately shown Franklin " in his far lesser lights: thrifty, domestic, dietarian, and, it may be, didactically waggish" (Ch. VIII).

96 Melville's ISRAEL POTTER

Melville clearly regards the Franklin philosophy as having been subverting, as if the man promised much to his country and delivered little. Franklin promises Israel his heart's desire, a return to home:

> "Well, I think I shall be able to procure you a passage." Israel's eyes sparkled with delight. The mild sage noticed it, and added: "But events in these times are uncertain. At the prospect of pleasure never be elated, but, without depression, respect the omens of ill. So much my life has taught me, my honest friend." Israel felt as though a plum-pudding had been thrust under his nostrils, and then as rapidly withdrawn (Ch. VII).

Franklin's long inquisition during their meal about how much bread may be bought for a bottle of wine (seventy-two penny rolls, in this case) is both a light parody of the Last Supper and reminiscent of the meetings of the Apostles of the Plinlimmon sect in Pierre:

> A tumbler of cold water was the utmost welcome to their reception rooms; at the grand supposed Sanhedrin presided over by one of the deputies of Plotinus Plinlimmon, a huge jug of Adam's Ale, and a bushel basket of Graham crackers were the only convivials (Bk. XXII, Chap. i).

But we know how Melville felt about crackers and water:

> Ah! ye poor lean ones! ye wretched Soakites and Vaporites! . . . attach the screw of your hose-pipe to some fine old butt of Madeira! pump us some sparkling wine into the world! see, see, already, from all eternity, two thirds of it have lain helplessly soaking ! (Ibid.).

Franklin, had not practiced what he so devotedly preached in Poor Richard and in his Autobiography. One historian reminds us that "he kept a negro page for his son, and had household slaves which his autobiography never mentions."[8] Another produces a more caustic indictment: "He spent money lavishly, ate so much that he suffered from gout for years and years, and when he was married at the age of twenty-four brought to his wife, as a wedding present, an illegitimate son."[9] But these were not important concerns in themselves for Melville.

What concerned Melville was the degree of moral sickness which he felt in the society of which he was a part, and whose most potent cause was the deforming and corrupting influence of the new industrialism; all of Israel Potter addresses itself to this sense of moral sickness, but where John Paul Jones is seen flying in retreat to an almost equally corrupting surrender to savagery and Ethan Allen is portrayed as thundering against it, Melville seems to place the burden of guilt at the feet of those corrupted by the legacy of Franklin. All the major artists of the day recorded that sense of moral sickness in their society. Hawthorne: "It sickens me to look back to America. I am sick to death of the continual fuss and tumult and excitement and bad blood which we keep up about political topics. . . . We are the most miserable people on earth."[10] Hawthorne was writing this in the same year that Melville was penning Israel Potter; as if to complement Melville's estimate of America as "civilized in externals but a savage at heart," Hawthorne thought that "the United States are fit for many excellent purposes, but they certainly are not fit to live in."[11] Surveying the political parties of the nation, Emerson could only conclude that "one has the best cause, and the other contains the best men"; unable to stand the heat, he had moved out of the kitchen.[12] Thoreau had stood his ground and fought, had gone to Walden and to jail. Melville, on the outer fringes of the political-literary alliance, had gone in these years nowhere but to his study, nursing the ideals of his "ruthless democracy," retreating slowly into a fashion of libertarian conservatism.

As Franklin plies Potter with apothegms dredged from Poor Richard, he is looting his room of all its little blessings, including the pretty maid. "Every time he comes in he robs me, . . . with an air all the time, too, as if he were making me presents" (Ch. IX). Again there is the disparity between promise and fulfillment, between the spirit of the apothegms and the practices of Franklin. When Melville makes his one sustained explicit attack on both the allegorical and historic Franklin, he scores his deceit and his comparative shallowness, his inability to so release himself as to be mastered passionately by any of the trades which he mastered. "Having carefully weighed the world, Franklin could act any part in it. By nature turned to knowledge, his mind was often grave, but never serious " (Ch. VIII), moving from field to field, being "printer, postmaster, almanac maker, . . . statesman, humorist, philosopher, parlor-man, political economist, professor of housewifery, . . .maxim-monger, herb-doctor, wit." His most crushing accusation is that "Franklin was everything but a poet." As Richard Chase pointed out, knowledge of The Confidence Man points out the "acid ambiguity" of some of the trades listed above. [13]

Franklin was not a poet and that, for Melville and Emerson, was a sin of incalculable magnitude. Unable to raise his head above the materialism of the earth, his virtues are all honed by the machinery of industrial development; industry and frugality are the greatest of these virtues;to be individualistic in the manner of Franklin is not to see the worth of the individual in relation to the macrocosmic forces which dominate the universe and against which the lone soul must brace itself, fortified by its sense of participation and spiritual dignity, but rather to pit individual against individual in an acquisitory struggle. 'Franklin, experimental, enquiring, discreetly bold, rationalistic, self-disciplined, was the personal embodiment of the capitalistic success, . . . the quintessence of eighteenth century liberalism."[14] But these were not the only attributes that Franklin possessed of which Melville could never become enthusiastic. If he noted that Franklin's style in literature was like that of Hobbes, " neat, trim, nothing superfluous, nothing deficient, . . . the paragon of perspicuity," it is comment enough to observe that these were literary qualities that Melville did not ever seek consciously to emulate.

Where Melville adored the sense of community among men, Franklin measured relationships too often against their value to him in his enterprises. "He played his human relationships as one hedges on the market, adapting quickly to changes and not raising the question of ultimate loyalties. . . . When family loyalty failed he became an isolated human being in a depersonalized world."[15] There is some of this sense of isolation in the portrait drawn by Melville; that picture is devoid of humanity and is in contrast to the booming vitality and gregariousness of Ethan Allen, even in captivity. All this stemmed from the absence in Franklin's soul of the transcendent impulses that could reject Mammon in favor of that unity of the ethical consciousness generically reflected in the arts, for Franklin's

Harpoon into Plowshare 99

materialism could never see the absolute need for a man who "stands among partial men for the complete men, and apprises us not of his wealth, but of the commonwealth."[16] This is Emerson in search of a definition of the true poet, and saying little with which Melville could disagree; the occasional attempts to read criticism of Emerson into this picture of Franklin in Israel Potter are, I think, not likely to be very fruitful. This is to overrate the general influence of Emerson in the 1850's or, indeed, at any time in the United States, as well as to underestimate the massiveness of the Franklin attitudes in comparison to any others. What Melville was striking against was less the man himself than all the new Ben Franklin's swarming over the United States of the redoubtable Bostonian. It is possible for one twentieth century historian to see Franklin's popularity in his day as

> probably a colossal misfortune to the United States, for, despite his good fellowship and occasional good sense, Franklin represented the least praiseworthy qualities of the inhabitants of the New World: miserliness, fanatical practicality, and lack of interest in what are usually known as spiritual things.... He extolled the virtues of honesty, industry, chastity, cleanliness and temperance--all excellent things. But it never occurred to him that with these alone life is not worth a fool's second thought. Philosophy, poetry, and the arts spring from different sources....[17]

Strong words. But these virtues of honesty, industry, chastity, cleanliness and temperance are precisely those outlined by Melville in the exchanges between Israel and Benjamin, and so acidly parodied.

Israel has become disenchanted with Giant Franklin; the meeting has yielded nothing, unless we count Franklin's gifts of a Guidebook to Paris and a copy of Poor Richard. Israel himself picks up the Pilgrim's Progress theme as he turns from one book to the other and finds both of little real significance, if not downright misleading:

> "So here is the 'Way to Wealth,' and here is the 'Guide to Paris.' Wonder now

whether Paris lies on the way to Wealth?
If so, I am on the road. More likely
though, it's a parting-of-the-ways (Ch.
IX).

In any event Israel leaves Giant Unprincipled Franklin and encounters on the way Giant Undaunted John Paul Jones. The link between the two mighty figures is a maxim of Franklin, which Jones reads and claims to have been his personal experience in life: "God helps them that help themselves"(Ch. XI). He is all self-reliance, as Franklin is:

"Dr. Franklin, whatever Paul Jones does for the cause of America, it must be done through unlimited orders; a separate, supreme command; no leader and no counsellor but himself. . . . I will mount, not sink. I live but for honor and glory . Give me, then, something honorable and glorious to do, and something famous to do it with" (Ch. X).

Franklin recognises a cousin and gives him what he wants.

But Melville's portrait of Jones is more sympathetically drawn, through there is a strain in it of ambiguity as Melville tries to reconcile under the aegis of approval the courage and charm of Jones with the egocentric pursuit of gloire that drives him like a madman up and down the seas. It is a difficult reconciliation because Melville suspects that both derive from the same source, a source that had no counterpart in the personality of Giant Franklin: the idea of a dynamism of primitivism and savagery that was unmistakeably American. Sharing the same room with Jones, and in a scene that finds Melville's alter-ego once again in the role of apprentice voyeur--watching another man undress--Israel sees "tattooing such as is seen only on thoroughbred savages" on the arm of "this barbarian in broad-cloth," whose rings and brooches,"not less than nose rings and tattooing, are tokens of the primeval savageness which ever slumbers in human kind." This quality of savagery was for Melville nothing to be unqualifiedly approved; what he could admire was pristine innocence, or primeval charm, not primitive scorn of the finer values of civilization; if there is a note of satire all through the following of Jones' campaign, there is a dead seriousness when the battle between the Bon Homme Richard and the Serapis gets underway and no approval once it is finished:

> In view of this battle one may ask -what separates the enlightened man from the savage? Is civilization a thing distinct, or is it an advanced state of barbarism?[18]

And the lesson for America is clearly drawn:

> Sharing the same blood with England, and yet her proved foe in two wars--not wholly inclined at bottom to forget an old grudge --intrepid, unprincipled, reckless, predatory, with boundless ambition, civilized in externals but a savage at heart, America is, or may yet be, the Paul Jones of nations (Ch. XIX).

Both at the personal and at the national level, this is warning. The progression of the soul and of the nation cannot be at the expense of humanity; it cannot be purely for the glory of self ; the Franklin brand of self-reliance, harnessed to the primitivism of the American national character, becomes reprehensible and dangerous. Only at the most superficial level is this a fight between Americans and the British, just as London stands for much more than the great city of England. Melville takes pains to reduce to essential minimum any idea of national partisanship; the English captain is a gentleman who concedes the fight and mercifully ends the carnage. "It is, therefore, honor to him as a man, and not reproach to him as an officer, that, to stay such carnage, Captain Pearson, of the Serapis, with his own hands hauled down his colors" (Ch. XIX). Melville's aim is not the description of national heroism.

His aim, instead, is the illumination of the dark, violent side of the American body. Thus he stresses that America shares the same blood as the English with whom Jones is fighting. The fight "seemed more like an intestine feud, than a fight between strangers. Or, rather, it was as if the Siamese Twins, oblivious of their fraternal bond, should rage in unnatural fight." Before half a decade had passed America was to be convulsed by the bitterest and most bloody intestinal feud in the history of nationhood, and if Melville did not predict the Civil war in Israel

Potter, as he did in the slightly later "Benito Cereno," he gave ample warning that all the ingredients of self-mutilation were present in the American national character as it endangered itself with such glorification and excuse of greed as was present, for example, in the concept of Manifest Destiny. For if Melville could depict violence in his writing, he was essentially a pacifist; his humanitarianism was too broad in its scope to admit an unequivocal sectional bias. When at last he published his poetry inspired by the conflict, both in verse and in prose he showed a pervading sadness at the loss mankind had suffered in this unnatural fight between Siamese Twins:

> Patriotism is not baseness, neither is it inhumanity. The mourners who this summer bear flowers to the mounds of the Virginian and Georgian dead are, in their domestic bereavement and proud affection, as sacred in the eye of Heaven as are those who go with similar offerings of tender offerings of grief and love into the cemetries of our Northern Martyrs.[19]

There is wide compassion and regret in his vision of 'the armies in the wilderness:"

> The May-weed springs; and comes a man
>   And mounts our Signal Hill;
> A quiet Man, and plain in garb--
>   Briefly he looks his fill,
> Then drops his gray eye on the ground,
>   Like a loaded mortar he is still:
> Meekness and grimness meet in him--
>   The silent general.
>
> Were men but strong and wise,
>   Honest as Grant, and calm,
> War would be left to the red and the black ants,
>   And the happy world disarm.[20]
> ("**Brute** Neighbors" Walden)

This echo in the last two lines of Thoreau should not let us forget that the prevailing note of regret stems from Melville's world-sorrow and hardly from any optative current in his world-view; the civil war may have disappointed Melville when at last it broke, but one suspects that it hardly surprised him until the horrors of mechanised warfare finally killed his long-ailing faith in a heroic tradition. Both in his craft of letters and in life, Melville had adjusted to the temper of his country in that decade of gathering storm in which he wrote his major works.

Primitivism fascinated Melville, an admirer of Rousseau. The tension between primitivism and the constraints of civilization is a continual theme in his work, from its beginnings in Typee, where it is explicitly described, through Moby Dick, "Benito Cereno" and beyond. In Israel Potter Melville does not unqualifiedly scorn the wilder elements in Jones' character; there is implicit sexual admiration as his Israel peers through the gloom at Jones' posturing before the mirror and cleansing himself at the wash-stand before lightly embracing the pretty chambermaid on his way out. "All barbarians," Melville tells us, "are rakes" (Ch. XI). And there is a merry pitting of Jones' eccentricity against the staid household of the Earl of Selkirk in Melville's parody of courtly traditions. But in the end John Paul Jones does nothing for Israel Potter but indirectly cause him to be abandonned on board the British man-of-war, where he is disowned by all. It is the last we hear of Jones; he has provoked one quarrel too many, as far as the journey of Israel is concerned. His erraticism almost seduces Potter, who seems to enjoy the company of the captain. Jones, and all that Jones stands for, offers Israel the lure of glory in the same way that Sir John Millet offered familial peace, King George offered position and Ben Franklin wealth. Though he is wary of following the Way to Wealth which Franklin provided, he seems undecided about the Path of Glory and ignorant about its general direction to the grave. Jones tries to get close to the young man: "You are a good, brave soul. You are the first among the millions of mankind that I ever naturally took to." Israel is not entirely blind; he sees Jones as a "lonely leader" (Ch. XXIV), and Jones is forced to concede that loneliness is part of the consequences of that dictum that God helps those who help themselves. Israel finally escapes from the temptation and leaves Jones and his heroic egotism far behind him in the wake of his progress; we soon see that Israel has not escaped unharmed.

Israel tries to find a place in the various little departments of the British battleship, but no one will accept him because no one has ever seen him before. It is too easily supposed that Melville is dramatising here only Israel's rejection by the world;

in fact, it is quite natural that Israel should have been rebuffed as he tried to insinuate himself into the various companies of men in different parts of the ship. More important is the fact that Israel so baffles the officers and men of the ship that he is set at liberty and eventually finds a secure place in the maintop. This is Israel's moment of triumph as confidence man and not the time of his rejection; subterfuge and brazen affirmations succeed for him against a representative sampling of the world; the world, for its part, has seen nothing like him:

> "He's out of all reason; out of all men's knowledge and memories! Why, no one knows him; no one has ever seen him before; no imagination, in the wildest flight of a morbid nightmare, has ever so much as dreamed of him. Who are you? . . . Are you down in the ship's books, or at all in the records of nature?" (Ch. XX).

Three times Israel Potter is asked his name and his origin. Three times Israel masquerades under the name of Peter Perkins and conceals the fact that he is American or a lover of liberty or the enemy of his country's enemies. There is no cock crowing thrice, but this is clearly Israel's moment of betrayal, the logical outcome of his exposure to the unprincipled selfishness of Franklin and Jones. Israel has shown in the past a small talent for escape and knows the value of changes of clothing, but his conduct aboard the battleship stands in marked contrast to the behaviour of the youth who stood up respectfully but firmly to an aristocrat and a king and refused to condemn the principles and people he held in esteem. That conduct on the ship works; Israel gains his place; but it has worked in the same way that Franklin's pettiness and Jones' savagery work: at the expense of ethical excellence, for which Israel will be punished. However dashing and spirited his performance as confidence man, he has committed a sacrilegious indiscretion in passing himself off as "a poor persecuted fellow," a Christ-like Peter, the rock upon which faith and principle rest; Israel is instead a rolling stone, with nothing to show for his journey so far through life.

Melville wastes no time between Israel's betrayal and his presentation of the ideal man, Ethan Allen. Israel coming upon Allen after his shameful performance on the battleship is not unlike Peter's shame-filled encounter with Christ after the third betrayal. "Arrived at the end of the arched-way, where the sun shone, Israel stood transfixed at the scene" where Allen is held captive. He does nothing. Melville had told us what Israel thought of Franklin and Jones and Sir John and the king, but we never know what goes through Israel's mind except apprehension, when he stands among the gaping spectators watching the magnificent defiance of Ethan Allen, his commanding figure, his assertion of principle, his courage, his inspired patriotism. Ethan Allen stands physically above his captors, "a martial man of Patagonian structure," but before long he is a man "towering . . . like a great whale," roaring "like some tormented lion," crouching "like some baited bull," whose "whole marred aspect was that of some wild beast; but of a royal sort; and unsubdued by the cage" (Ch. XXI). A visiting Lady thinks this "wild, mossed American from the woods" is particularly impressive, with his "leopard-like teeth," and, annoyed by some soldier, Allen is soon "turning like a tiger." His manner is "scornful and ferocious in the last degree." The idea of primitive force is stressed; indeed, at no other point of the book does Melville have recourse to such accumulation of animal images as when he describes Ethan Allen. All this time, Allen is dressed, not in the affected manner of Franklin or Jones, but in "the sorry remains of a half-Indian half-Canadian sort of dress, consisting of a fawn-skin jacket--the fur outside and hanging in ragged tufts--a half- rotten, barklike belt of wampum."[21]

But this is a primitivism different from that displayed by John Paul Jones. It stems not from vanity but from a sense of identification with the natural innocence of the American west. Allen had become in Melville's eyes the finest expression of the finest spirit of the country; more than this, there was the thread of universality in the man. His European stock is cosmopolite, "a curious combination of a Hercules, a Joe Miller, a Bayard and a Tom Hyer; had a person like the Belgian giants; mountain music in him like a Swiss; a heart plump as Coeur de Leon's. "Unlike Jones, he mixes the most attractive elements of the primitive character with the best of the European. He is as "companionable as a Pagan." Where Jones was the lonely leader, Allen is representative of the kind of man and the philosophy of life that Melville most admired and sought in his countrymen over all others. Melville must have been conscious that his own life was, in a sense, more like Israel's, scurrying around in various disguises, pursued by Fate. Ethan Allen sometimes bargained or bragged, but he stood his ground and did battle in the face of overwhelming odds and almost certain and ignominious death. All the while, though, Allen was motivated by the loftiest ideals, and those which Melville himself most dearly cherished: frankness, conviviality, honor and brotherhood. It was what Melville sought in his country and his countrymen, but not with much hope; Jones and Franklin seemed both, in their separate ways, to be carrying the day; "if in this book Melville seems at one point to fear that America may yet become the John Paul Jones of nations, in The Confidence Man he seems to find it far more likely that America will become the Benjamin Franklin of nations."[22] Allen embodied the Western spirit and was thus peculiarly American, "for the Western spirit is, or will yet be (for no other is, or can be), the true American one" (Ch. XXII).

Israel stands in the crowd and watches Giant Unconquerable Ethan Allen and dares not reveal himself; he is moved, however, to visit some Americans in prison. He is loudly hailed by a prisoner. Israel denies again his identity; he "was no Yankee rebel, thank Heaven, but a true man to his king" (Ch. XXII). In the Life and Remarkable Adventures the real Potter had had a similar experience; he was able to leave some money for the prisoners after easily denying his identity. Melville's Israel has to deny his identity to escape not only a sentry but also a suspicious board of officers, and is released only after much scrutiny. He abandons the battleship, which is tied up near Allen's place of captivity, because of rumours of impressments, and plunges on towards London, the powerful voice of Allen ringing misunderstood in his ears. It is some time before he gets to London. In the Life and Remarkable Adventures, Potter's work in the brickyards had taken place in London and only during the summer months over a period of five years. Melville moves the scene out of London so that it is on the way of Potter's grand progress, and he has Israel working for "thirteen weary weeks" (Ch. XXII). In those thirteen weary weeks Israel reaches the lowest point of his moral life, as he surrenders himself to the desecrating processes that destroy the earth's natural life-giving capacity though fire in the blazing kilns. Israel has sold himself to the forces of soulless industrialism; nowhere does he come closer to despair. The burning of the earth warns of the coming desolation of Israel in the brick-built City of Dis.

Chapter Six

Requiescat in Pace

When Israel leaves the side of Ethan Allen, his progress is almost at an end, but there are still signposts on the road. He has proved himself unable to respond effectively to the challenge posed by Allen largely because he does not quite understand what Allen stands for and the necessity of his defiance. For others it might be obvious; for Israel, perhaps culpably ignorant, it is elusive. When the time comes for him to work in the brickyards, there is another bold message to be understood in all the slapping and splashing and baking; Israel this time partly grasps the significance of his occupation. The chapter is crucial to the novel's success; it is not only a stunning display of Melville's command of chiaroscuro but also vital to the symbolic unity of the novel, presenting the major antithetical response to the positive philosophical themes deriving from the novel as a complete work. Where the earth looms large at the start of the novel in the sweeping panorama of Israel's birthplace and recurs at the end of the book, when the mysterious p l o w m a n turns up with his p l o w the remnants of the old Potter home, here in the brickyard scene Melville stages the repudiation of his major theme; here mother earth is not sexually united with her sons in the ordained incest of plowing; rather it is the victim of an unspeakable matricide by which the city's rise and man's materialism is measurable. Israel's part in this crime matches the desertion of home that first sends him on his way in repudiation of the soil and daily, honorable labor. The crime is not without rewards, apart from the obvious financial gain. In fact, there are two lessons to be learnt; Israel, as always, does not understand them both.

He does gain from the mechanical slapping and splashing that is his assignment what all the other workers in the brickyard soon find out: the utter vanity of a world in which men and bricks are both no more than lumps of clay fashioned in the hands of a brickmaker and destined to crumble and return to the dust from which they came. "To these muddy philosophers, men and bricks were equally of clay. 'What signifies who we be--dukes or ditchers?' thought the mounders; 'all is vanity and clay.' So slap, slap, slap, care-free and negligent, with bitter unconcern, these dismal desperadoes flapped down the dough" (Ch. XXIII). It is the lesson of Ecclesiastes that Melville knew so well; the comparison between this brickyard scene and the Tryworks chapter of Moby Dick finds Melville in the same mood when faced with another earth-grown microcosm of the fires of hell. Melville as an author hardly ever wastes anything; if in the Tryworks chapter "the sun hides not Virginia's Dismal Swamp," in the brickyard scene in Israel Potter cleanliness in as impossible as with a man "at the bottom of the lake in the Dismal Swamp." This is not the only example of Melville's literary economy in comparing the two chapters; indeed, the brickyard writing shows how far Melville had come in command of restraint and the judicious exercise of power. But the lesson of both chapters is in one important way alike. Ecclesiastes casts the long shadow. "The truest of all men was the Man of Sorrows, and the truest of all books is Solomon's, and Ecclesiastes is the fine-hammered steel of woe. All is vanity. ALL " (Moby Dick, Ch. XCVI).

In both chapters there is a vital qualification, which Israel epitomizes in his ignorant refusal to fall into despair. Though he joins the crowd of workers in the conclusion that all is vanity in the world, by his action he does not pursue the logical implications of that statement, which can only tend to negate the life-force and life-purpose, and, ultimately, life itself. In Moby Dick Melville instructs us not to surrender to the miseries of the world and despair, though all be vanity; "Give not thyself up, then, to fire, lest it invert thee, deaden thee, as far as the time it did me. There is a wisdom that is woe; but there is a woe that is madness." Out of unhappiness, Melville is saying, comes wisdom, but out of wisdom, more unhappiness, and from too much unhappiness comes not more wisdom, but self-destruction. There is enough positivism here to indicate that Melville even then had been able to recognise the naivete of "an empty innocence, a tenacious ignorance of evil, which, granted the tough nature of reality, must be either immaturity or spiritual cowardice," as R. W.B. Lewis says. There is also enough positivism here to indicate that Melville already understood what he further explores in Israel Potter, that evil must be resisted at the same time that it is acknowledged, and that to surrender to the hypnosis of evil over the potential of good is to ensure self-destruction. This is not Transcendental optimism; it is too basically a kit for survival. Israel Potter further illustrates the progression of Melville "beyond both innocence and despair to some glimmering of a moral order," as Lewis says. This is the meaning of Melville's parable of the bricks in Israel Potter, beyond even the psychological implications of the dehumanisation effects of such work, expressed differently elsewhere in the "Tartarus of Maids." The prime concern in Israel Potter and at this point of the book is more fundamental to the Melville view of life; for each man is a brick and life is a fiery kiln in which all are placed; the quality of each life varies in a strange way with the closeness of the flame:

> The bricks immediately lining the vaults would be all burnt to useless scrolls, black as charcoal, and twisted into shapes the most grotesque; the next tier would be a little less withered, but hardly fit for service; and gradually, as you went higher and higher. . . you came to the midmost ones, sound, square, and perfect bricks, bringing the highest prices; from these the contents of the kiln gradually deteriorated in the opposite direction, upward. . . . The summit ones were pale with the languor of too exclusive an exemption from the burden of the blaze (Ch. XXIII).

Somewhere in the middle, neither consumed by the vicissitudes of life nor unexposed to them, man finds salvation on earth. Israel is as close to the flame as one human brick can go, but he never becomes either useless or grotesque. Though Israel seems to Melville a gravedigger as he ladles the dough into the mould s and passes them on, there are two sides to this graveyard work; even as he tucks away "dead little innocents in their coffins on one side," he is also "cunningly disinterring them again to resurrectionists stationed on the other."

    The secondary, anti-industrial theme should not be ignored. It assumes great significance in retrospect when Melville enters the city of London, his hoped-for Celestial City, his actual City of Destruction. He is wise enough to see the irony of his work in the brickyards: that he is helping to build, almost as an old Israeli slave, the very nation that he opposes. The fuller implication would strike him once he recognises the grand disillusionment of the city and its devastation of humanity; Israel shares in the guilt for it all, for both as brickmaker and as human being he sees London and this perversion of the human spirit as happening in a house that he partially built. As he crosses the bridge into London, bewildered by the inhumanity of the scene, "Israel's heart was prophetically heavy; foreknowing, that being of this race, felicity could never be his lot " (Ch. XXIV).

    "Being of this race." Here is the complete submerging of the national aspect of Israel's story, and the emerging of the fuller human implication of the travails and triumphs of Melville's Pilgrim. The question of the true American spirit or the danger of materialism or of primitive urgings towards violence in the American character deal with a fundamental subject at a level necessarily high to be able to encompass both individualistic and national and supra-national meaning. In such an arrangement there is compromise that lessens the impact of the novel as a document of the individual search; Melville has moved consistently to rectify this and at the end of the novel so manipulates his symbolic apparatus that the individual clearly comes into focus as the matter of nation recedes. Israel makes his pathetic return to the home of his fathers after being almost run over by a patriotic triumphal car in a Fourth of July procession. On that vulgar note Melville separates the embodiment of American mass humanity from the pilgrim who is also Everyman. Behind Israel at this point lies more than half a century of adventure, misfortune, deprivation and near-despair, encounters with the great and near-great, with a king and with counsellors, with hallucinations and dreams. This is the legacy with which he returns to his father's home; that home is gone. The first sign of the old order is also the indication of finality: a half-cord of hemlock wood turning to dust but holding still its exact look unless prodded by a passer-by. The message of that hemlock is that death is impending; old Israel and the pile of logs from his youth are together approaching the return to dust.

    The family has vanished, gone West. Israel would have gone with them if he had stayed within the fold. Melville does not mention that Israel has lost his share of the legacy; his fiction is that the whole family, father and all, have gone west following the American sun while Israel has moved erratically east, misled by false gods and his own ignorance. Yet we know nothing really of that family and we have followed Israel in his progress; Israel looms as a figure that has passed through the kiln of life, and his scars and burns are not without honor. For Israel himself it is a moment of revelation. The very house in which he was born has passed from the earth; there would have been no trace of it had not the plowman working dutifully in the fields unearthed the hearthstone of the lost house of Potter. When he had made in his youth the step that put him firmly on the road away from home, the call had found him at the plow (Ch. III). When he receives here what must be the final call to home, he is again beside the plow. The last two sentences spoken by Israel Potter summarize the lessons of his life as he turns away with his one son from the side of the plowman: "The ends meet. Plough away, friend." In less than a dozen lines, Melville closes the book.

    Too late in <u>Pierre</u> Melville realized that he was telling a fatally unrelieved <u>tale</u> full of maudlin sentimentality and affected language; he almost hurriedly sought to counterbalance these errors of judgment by recourse to a kind of humor more sarcastic than satiric and, in the end, no laughing matter at all. In <u>Israel Potter</u> Melville made no such mistake; he had the additional responsibility to the magazine readership. His deployment of comic sequence and tone in <u>Israel Potter</u> is the finest in all his work.

    The humor in <u>Israel Potter</u> is primarily a comedy of terrors. There is some harmless parody and restrained satire, but the overwhelming impact is achieved by the sustained comic rendering of the terrifying. It is the functional counterpoint of the serious journey towards the City of Destruction that Israel is making. Melville uses these incidents of terror to sustain both the comic spirit and the notion of Israel's wanderings as a journey through a forbidding place where pitfalls are everywhere ready to destroy the unsuspecting traveller. The lightness of touch and tone that distinguishes Melville's portrayal of Franklin and Jones are not necessarily a part of this method; it should be noticed that the same lightness of tone and touch disappears from the novel almost completely after the Serapis and the Bon Homme Richard approach to do battle, reappearing only with Israel's attempts to deceive the officers and men on board the British battleship. Part of what might be called this primary level of comedy in Israel Potter are such passages of parody as Jones' attempts to burn the town of Whitehaven, when the party of dashing heroes forgets to bring matches and are forced to borrow some fire from an irate townsman, as well as the courtly looting of the Selkirk mansion, where the lady cooperates with the castle stormers and allows servants to assist the bungling party (Chs. XVI & XVII). These are Melville's adaptations of historically verifiable incidents; his comedy of terrors is of his own invention.

The comedy involving the terrifying represents a continual harassment of Israel's perceptive faculties both visually and intellectually. He is too often too blind through his own ignorance to see the wood for the trees. There are other occasions when he seems to have learnt the lesson of reality and apparition and is even able to turn the tables on the world. His changes of clothing and general deceptive ability are consistently mocked by these more powerful forces that dog him on the road. They are leading him in as disparate directions as the Franklin, Jones and Allen appeals. The harassment begins almost simultaneously with Israel's departure from home, at the Battle of Bunker hill, though the incidents are never again quite as gruesome. Israel sees a blade "horizontally menacing his feet from the ground," and tries to wrench the steel from the hand holding the blade. There is a strange force at work grasping the sword; "it was some British officer's laced sword-arm, cut from the trunk in the act of fighting, refusing to yield up its blade to the last" (Ch. III). This is not a very amusing incident, but it predicts in Israel Potter forces at work in which Israel is hard pressed to contend.

In the same chapter, Israel finds himself in England, after having escaped from his captors; standing in a field, he is moved to tears by the beauty of the scenery: "He was so sad, and these sights were so gay, that Israel sobbed like a child, while thoughts of his mountain home rushed like a wind on his heart." Soon he meets two persons working in the fields. In talking to them he believes that they are ladies because of their peculiar dress: they, in turn, are both annoyed at his mistake and bovine in their stupidity. Israel seeks the way to London; they merely send him on his way without a hint of direction; "having now satisfied their rustic curiosity, the two human steers, with wonderful phlegm, applied themselves to their hoes." Israel has received a warning here as he seeks to find the way to his Celestial City; the very next lines, describing a place never mentioned in the <u>Life and Remarkable Adventures</u>, bring into the novel a new element of decadence and religious fall to which Melville will return in the entombment scene and later in the brickyard and the City of Dis: leaving the two "human steers,"

> Israel passed an old, dark, mossy-looking chapel, its roof all plastered with the damp yellow dead leaves of the previous autumn, showered there from a close cluster of venerable trees, with great trunks, and overstretching branches (Ch. III).

Before chapter three ends, Melville again introduces disquieting influences under the loose guise of comedy as Melville broadly parodies the Biblical healing scenes where the lame are made to walk and throw away their crutches. Pretending to be crippled, Israel is given a ride by a wagon driver as he continues on the way to London; "but after a time, finding the gait of the elephantine draught-horses intolerably slow, Israel craves permission to dismount, when, throwing away his crutch, he takes nimbly to his legs, much to the surprise of his honest friend the driver."

There is the same measure of the grotesque and the ridiculous mixed in Israel's flirtation with the bottle of "Otard," which he almost consumes before Ben Franklin informs him of its meaning and contents and removes the bottle of poison from his room, along with several other commodities which Franklin treats with equal circumspection. But the most formidable combination of terror and comedy comes with the concealment of Israel by Squire Woodcock in the old Templar hiding place, and Israel's subsequent escape from the home dressed in the dead squire's clothing. Again Melville uses the occasion to prefigure the suffering and rejection of Israel, for as he grows more and more despondent in the enclosed space of the cell, "suddenly, as if some strange contagious fever had seized him, he was afflicted with strange enchantments of misery, undreamed of till now " (Ch. XII). There is the assault through terror on the physical and psychological processes by which Israel lives: "The delirious sense of the absence of light was soon added to his other delirium as to the contraction of space. The lids of his eyes burst with impotent distension." The whole weight of the world seems to be pressing upon him as Israel lies concealed in the tiny room; he is oppressed by the "sense of being masoned up in the wall, . . . as if vast blacks of stone had been laid on him." There is a dead seriousness about all this, a certainty that the process witnessed in the symbolic entombment of the central character; yet when he emerges from the cell and dresses himself in all the finery of the dead man and makes his escape, the whole process is startlingly reversed. The abused has become the abuser; if Israel's escape is a genial parody of the Christian Resurrection, then all of the Christian community are at one with the petrified and deluded members of the Squire's household as Israel passes in disguise before their eyes:

> He advanced with a slow and stately step, looked neither to the right nor the left, but went solemnly forward on his now faintly illuminated way, sounding his cane on the floor as he passed. The faces in the doorways curdled his blood by their rooted looks. Glued to the spot, they seemed incapable of motion. As he passed the lady in the widow's weeds, she fell senseless and crosswise before him. But forced to be immutable in his purpose, Israel, solemnly stepping over her prostrate form, marched deliberately on (Ch. XIII).

Liberated by these almost sacrilegious means, Israel marches boldly out before the mansion into the open fields when suddenly "he saw a man in black standing right in his path. . . . To the brooding soul of the now desolate Israel, so strange a sight roused a supernatural suspicion." The tables are again turned; it is Israel's turn to be subject to hallucination and terror stemming from inadequacy of perception; the man in black is simply a scarecrow. Back and forth Melville takes his repeated inversions of the roles of deceiver and deceived, as Israel soon attempts to inflict on a suspicious farmer the kind of a terror visited on him by the scarecrow. Israel runs briskly to the identical spot where the scarecrow had stood (he is now wearing the clothes of the stuffed man, the hollow man) and pretends to be something not alive. The farmer is wary, but a hardy type; he will test the validity of this apparition with the reality of his pitchfork. Israel, for a while, makes a brave showing of it. "At last the man slowly presented one prong of his fork towards Israel's left eye. Nearer and nearer the sharp point came, till no longer capable of enduring such a test, Israel took to his heels with all speed, his tattered coat-tails streaming behind him." Soon after, in the same chapter, a bull dog takes after the harassed Israel, tearing a t his coat, chewing at his hat; "not only was his coat a mere rag, but his breeches, clawed by the dog, were slashed into yawning gaps, while his yellow hair waved over the top of the crownless beaver, like a lonely tuft of heather on the highlands."

All this might appear too close to farce to be truly useful in a serious allegorical quest, but one has only to turn to a work like Piers Ploughman to find a very similar juxtaposition of the farcical with the mildly satirical, the humorlessly didactic with sustained inspiration. Both Langland and Melville are masters of the comic effect; both display their skill side by side w i t h serious intent, as comedy and tragedy are side by side in the natural world: in Piers Ploughman, "the poem sometimes swings back and forth between extremes; harsh prophecy or solemn warnings, and Rabelaisian satire that is not afraid to expose contradictions in terms of farce."[1] We have that same adventurous mixture in Israel Potter, even if there is a greater coherence in Melville than in Langland's poem. This adventuresome quality is capable of deceiving even astuter critics. In Israel Potter, i t has contributed in great measure to the low critical standing of the work, even in the face of the twentieth century revaluation of the Melville canon: in Piers Ploughman, down to the present time, understandment of the work has been retarded "by the largely groundless assumption that Langland wrote carelessly and was no artist."[2]

In many respects Israel Potter is second only to Moby Dick among Melville's longer works. Investigations of Pierre, Mardi or The Confidence-Man are, to varying extents, autopsies; however stimulating certain aspects of each prove to be in a study of Melville as a complete artist, none of those works satisfies in itself the requirements that an individual work of art, to be successful, should exist as a specimen of unity, beauty and significance, autonomous of any other consideration. In all three, the reader must look before and after and pine for what is not at the moment before his eyes. Talk continually revolves around the lessons of Melville's grand failures or rich promise ahead. Israel Potter stands in relation to all other works of Melville by nature of their common paternity, but it stands by itself in its ability to succeed and impress upon the reader the intentions of the author.

It is a complex work. It exists on multiple levels as comedy, tragedy, didactic moral allegory, poem of consolation, picaresque adventure, even quasi-epic. It addresses itself to questions of ultimate destiny and man's relation to the forces at work impeding his progress towards the realisation of that rendezvous with significance without which life is quite meaningless. It is a work that simultaneously spurns despair and rejects social, religious or economic liberalism. It is shot through with a gripping artistic and ideological honesty, and it stands among the works of Melville as the most complete statement of the responsibilities and rewards of the common man in his sojourn in this vale of tears. It looks back for its literary antecedents not to the shallow neo-Gothic processes or the spiritually compromising heroic epic, but instead to a wealth of literature whose primary aim has been always the moral edification of humanity. Dealing with the qualities of patriotism, it betrays no parochial bias, but speaks to all nations whose ideals, lofty in conception, are being eroded in practice; as religious in tone as anything Melville ever wrote, it recommends no ecclesiastical panacea and burns no heretics; it harks back, instead, to a medieval certitude in the attainment of spiritual sufficiency through adherence to the duties of the common life.

<u>Israel Potter</u> is, in final effect, a dream poem as surely as the medieval allegories were almost inevitably dream poems. Melville does not hasten to tell us this because he has sensed that this particular time of his career was inopportune for such demonstrative artistic innovation. The fantastic occurrences of Potter's life, the fight at Bunker Hill, the meeting with King George, with Ethan Allen, with Ben Franklin and John Paul Jones, the spanning of oceans and the final return to home, all are suffused in the mists of reverie, though the mists vary in opaqueness as glints of realism cut through the gloom. It is Melville's way of explaining such fortuitous circumstances; life, after all, is a dream:

> "Do I dream?" mused the bewildered old
> man, "or what is that vision that comes
> to me of a cold, cloudy morning, long,
> long ago, and I heaving yon elbowed log
> against the beech, then a sapling. Nay,
> nay, I cannot be so old " (Ch. XXVI).

<u>Israel Potter</u> is the dream-vision of a community's master artist

looking steadily out of his study-window at a nation and a world which though consistently rebuking his efforts to aid them is unable to subjugate his indomitable spirit.

NOTES

Chapter One

[1] *Life and Remarkable Adventures of Israel R. Potter* (New York, 1962), with an introduction by Leonard Kriegel, is the most recent reprinting of this work. This 1962 Corinth Books publication is the text used in this study; in notation it will be referred to as *Life*. Potter's narrative has also been reprinted in the *Magazine of History* and, in abridged form, in *America Rebels: Narratives of the Patriots*, ed. Richard M. Dorson (New York, 1953).

[2] J. Howard and Henry Trumbull, in 1824. The title pages of both printings are reproduced in the Corinth Books edition. Trumbull wrote and published the book (*Life*, p. viii).

[3] See title pages in *Life*.

[4] Jay Leyda, *The Melville Log* (New York, 1951), I, 315.

[5] Leyda, I, 350.

[6] Leyda, I, 378.

[7] Leyda, I, 378.

[8] To Lemuel Shaw, October 6, 1849. *The Letters of Herman Melville*, eds. Merrill R. Davis and William H. Gilman (New Haven, 1960), 91.

[9] Dedication, "To His Highness The Bunker-Hill Monument," June, 17th 1854, in Herman Melville's *Israel Potter* (New York, 1855).

[10] F. O. Matthiessen, *American Renaissance* (New York, 1941), 489.

[11] Hugh W. Hetherington, *Melville's Reviewers* (Chapel Hill, 1961), 192.

[12] Hetherington, 231.

[13] Hetherington, 218.

[14] Newton Arvin, Herman Melville (New York, 1950), 200.

[15] Hetherington, 237.

[16] Nathaniel Hawthorne, The English Notebook, ed. Randall Stewart (New York, 1962), 432.

[17] Leyda, I, 469.

[18] Leyda, I, 469f.

[19] Arvin, 198-199.

[20] Victor Wolfgang Von Hagen, Introduction to The Encantadas (Burlingame, California, 1940), p. v.

[21] Ibid.

[22] Ibid.

[23] Matthiessen, 491.

[24] Arvin, 231.

[25] Matthiessen, 421-431.

[26] Emilio Cecchi, " Two notes on Herman Melville," Sewanee Review, LXVIII, 403.

[27] Ibid.

120 Melville's ISRAEL POTTER

Chapter Two

[1] Leyda, I, 490.

[2] Leyda, II, 499.

[3] Leyda, II, 501.

[4] Leyda, II, 504.

[5] Hetherington, 245.

[6] Hetherington, 247.

[7] Ibid.

[8] Darrel Abel, American Literature (Woodbury, New York, 1963), II, 424.

[9] Marcus Cunliffe, The Literature of the United States (Baltimore, 1967), 125.

[10] John Bernstein, Pacifism and Rebellion in the Writings of Herman Melville (London, 1964), 147.

[11] Matthiessen, 492.

[12] Arvin, 245.

[13] Richard Chase, Herman Melville (New York, 1948), 176.

[14] Yvor Winters, In Defence of Reason (New York, 1947), 233.

[15] Edward H. Rosenberry, "Israel Potter, Benjamin Franklin and the Doctrine of Self Reliance," Emerson Society Quarterly, No. 28, Part 3 (1962), 27.

[16] Leyda, I, 489.

[17] Leyda, I, 449.

[18] Merton M. Sealts, Melville as Lecturer (Cambridge, Mass., 1957), 119.

[19] Dedication, Israel Potter.

[20] Ibid.

[21] Ibid.

[22] Bernstein, 147.

[23] Richard M. Dorson, ed., America Rebels: Narratives of the Patriots (New York, 1953), 14.

[24] Leonard Kriegel, Introduction to Life, p. vi.

[25] These two passages were among those selected for comparison in Roger P. McCutcheon's "The Technique of Melville's Israel Potter," South Atlantic Quarterly, XXVII (April 1928), 161-174.

[26] Arvin, 246.

[27] It is no reflection on Melville's skill to remember that he turned to sources other than Life for several of these greatly admired passages. Melville's borrowing has been documented by W. Sprague Holden in his unpublished master's thesis, "Some sources for Herman Melville's Israel Potter," Columbia University, 1932, and more recently by Walter Dickinson Jones in his unpublished doctoral dissertation, "A critical study of Herman Melville's Israel Potter," at the University of Alabama in 1963. Melville's principal sources other than Life were Robert G. Sands' Life and Correspondence of John Paul Jones (New York, 1830), James Fenimore Cooper's History of the Navy, John Henry Sherburne's Life and Character of the Chevalier John Paul Jones

122 Melville's ISRAEL POTTER

(City of Washington, 1825), and Ethan Allen's <u>Narrative of Colonel Ethan Allen's Captivity</u> (Philadelphia, 1779).

[28] Sealts, 34.

Chapter Three

[1] Leyda, I, 461.

[2] Leyda, II, 507.

[3] Leyda, I, 488.

[4] There are other references to magazine writing in <u>Pierre</u> and they also seem to indicate that his opinion of the literary medium was not always high. Book XVIII, Chap. i: "Inasmuch as by various indirect intimations much more than ordinary natural genius has been imputed to Pierre, it may have seemed an inconsistency, that only the merest magazine papers should have been thus far the sole productions of his mind." In Chapter two of that same Book, describing Pierre's fellow contributors to the Gazell Magazine: ". . . their lives had all been fraternally written by each other, and they had clubbed, and had their likenesses all taken by the aggregate job, and published on paper, all bought at one shop."

[5] Leyda, I, 488.

[6] Matthiessen, 491.

[7] Robert M. Farnsworth, "<u>Israel Potter</u>: Pathetic Comedy," <u>Bulletin of the New York Public Library</u>, <u>LXV</u> (1961), 125.

[8] Harry Levin, <u>The Power of Blackness</u> (New York, 1958), 191.

[9] To Nathaniel Hawthorne, 1 June, 1851. <u>Letters</u>, eds. Merrell and Gilman, 130.

Chapter Four

[1] Russel A. Peck, ed., Confessio Amantis (New York, 1968), xi-xii.

[2] The Pearl, translated by Sister Mary Vincent Hillmann (Notre Dame, 1961), 5.

[3] Attributed to "a great Melville scholar" by David E. Smith, John Bunyan in America (Bloomington, Indiana), p. vii. Professor Smith's discussion of the influence of Bunyan on Hawthorne and other American authors and his research into Bunyan's more direct American imitators leave me much indebted to him.

[4] Quoted by David E. Smith, 17.

[5] David E. Smith, 21.

[6] David E. Smith, 26.

[7] Henry Nash Smith, Virgin Land (New York, 1950), p. 85.

[8] Henry Nash Smith, 85-86.

[9] Isaiah (19:18): "In that day shall five cities in the land of Egypt speak the language of Canaan, and swear to the LORD of hosts; one shall be called, the City of Destruction. Christian flees the City of Destruction, the place of his birth, at the urging of Evangelist": John Bunyan, Pilgrim's Progress, ed. James Blanton Wharey (2nd ed.; London, 1960), 11.

[10] Pilgrim's Progress, 162.

[11] Pilgrim's Progress, 156.

[12] Pilgrim's Progress, 157.

[13] Pilgrim's Progress, 124.

[14] David E. Smith, 14.

[15] David E. Smith, 48.

[16] Pilgrim's Progress, 98.

[17] Pilgrim's Progress, 157.

[18] Ibid.

[19] Pilgrim's Progress, 158.

Chapter Five

[1] John T. Frederick, "Symbol and Theme in Melville's Israel Potter," Modern Fiction Studies, VIII, iii (Autumn 1962), 268.

[2] Ray B. Browne's "Israel Potter: Metamorphosis of Superman," in Ray B. Browne et alia, eds., Frontiers of American Culture (Lafayette, Indiana, 1968), 89.

[3] Life, 30.

[4] William Langland, Piers the Ploughman, trans. J. F. Goodridge (Baltimore, 1966), 81.

[5] For forty-five years Piers follows the goddess Fortune and the two ladies in her train called Lust-of-the-Flesh and Lust-of-the-Eyes. Goodridge, 127-129.

[6] Goodridge, 185.

[7] Goodridge, 231.

[8] Gladys Meyer, "The Urban Pattern of Success," in Charles L. Sanford, ed., Benjamin Franklin and the American Character (Boston, 1955), 50.

⁹Charles Angoff, "Benjamin Franklin," in <u>Benjamin Franklin and the American Character</u>, 53.

¹⁰Arvin, 208.

¹¹Ibid.

¹²Arthur M. Schlesinger, Jr., <u>The Age of Jackson</u> (Boston, 1945), 385.

¹³Chase, 180.

¹⁴Meyer, 51.

¹⁵Ibid.

¹⁶Ralph Waldo Emerson, "The Poet."

¹⁷Angoff, 53-54.

¹⁸Melville was drawing heavily here and throughout the long battle between the two ships from a letter written by John Paul Jones to Benjamin Franklin and quoted in Charles Sands' <u>Life and Correspondence of John Paul Jones</u> and John Henry Sherburne's <u>The Life and Character of the Chevalier John Paul Jones</u>; for a clear account of the debt, see Jack Russell, "<u>Israel Potter</u> and 'Song of Myself', "<u>American Literature</u>, XL, i(March 1968), 72-76. Melville is obviously recasting the picture of Jones, for far from being callous about the fight, Jones had written to Franklin: "A person must have been an eye-witness to form a just idea of the tremendous scene of carnage, wreck, and ruin that everywhere appeared. Humanity cannot but recoil from the prospect of such finished horror, and lament that war should produce such fatal consequences." Melville barely modifies Jones' words, but we never suspect that Jones originally penned them.

¹⁹Supplement to <u>Battle Pieces</u>.

[20] Melville's "Armies of the Wilderness" (lines 123-134), Battle-Pieces and Aspects of the War (New York, 1866).

[21] The Narrative of Colonel Ethan Allen, published in 1779 and most recently reprinted by Corinth Books (New York, 1961), gives Allen's own account of his dress: "A few days before I was taken in a Canadian dress, viz. a short fawn skin jacket, double-breasted, an under vest and breeches of sagathy, worsted stockings, a decent pair of shoes, two plain shirts, and a red worsted cap; this was all the clothing I had, in which I made my appearance in England" (p. 36).

[22] Farnsworth, 129.

Chapter Six

[1] Goodridge, 13.

[2] Goodridge, 11.

A Selected Bibliography for Melville's Israel Potter

Allen, Ethan. Narrative of Col. Ethan Allen's Captivity. New York, 1961.

Arvin, Newton. Herman Melville. New York, 1950

Browne, Ray B. "Israel Potter: Metamorphosis of Superman," Frontiers of American Culture, eds. Ray B. Browne, Richard H. Crowder, Virgil L. Lokke and William T. Stafford. Lafayette, Indiana, 1968.

Cecchi, Emilio. "Two notes on Herman Melville," Sewanee Review, LXVIII (Summer, 1960), 398-406.

Chase, Richard. "Israel in the Wilderness," Herman Melville. New York, 1949.

Cooper, James Fenimore. History of the Navy, 1839.

Farnsworth, Robert M. "Israel Potter: Pathetic Comedy," Bulletin of the New York Public Library, LXV (February 1961), 125-132.

Frederick, John T. "Symbol and Theme in Melville's Israel Potter," Modern Fiction Studies, VIII, iii (Autumn 1962), 265-275.

Gross, John J. "The Face of Plinlimmon and the 'Failures' of the Fifties," Emerson Society Quarterly, No. 28, Part 3 (1962), 6-9.

_____. Herman Melville and the Search for Community. Unpublished manuscript.

Hetherington, Hugh W. Melville's Reviewers. Chapel Hill, 1961.

Holden, W. Sprague. "Some sources for Herman Melville's Israel Potter," Unpublished master's thesis, Columbia University, 1932.

Hull, Raymona. "London and Melville's Israel Potter," Emerson Society Quarterly, No. 47, 78-81.

Jackson, Kenny. "Israel Potter; Melville's Fourth of July Story," College Language Association Journal, VI, iii (March 1963), 194-204.

Jones, Walter Dickinson. "A Critical Study of Herman Melville's Israel Potter." Unpublished doctoral dissertation, University of Alabama, 1963.

Leyda, Jay. The Melville Log. 2 vols. New York, 1951.

McCutcheon, Roger P. "The Technique of Melville's Israel Potter," South Atlantic Quarterly, XXVII, ii (April 1928), 161-174.

Matthiessen, F. O. American Renaissance. New York, 1941.

Melville, Herman. Israel Potter. New York, 1855.

Potter, Israel R. Life and Remarkable Adventures of Israel R. Potter. New York, 1962.

Rosenberry, Edward H. "Israel Potter, Benjamin Franklin and the Doctrine of Self Reliance," Emerson Society Quarterly, No. 28, Part 3 (1962), 27-30.

Russell, Jack. "Israel Potter and 'Song of Myself'," American Literature, XL, i (March 1968), 72-76.

Sands, Robert F. Life and Correspondence of John Paul Jones. New York, 1830.

Sherburne, John Henry. Life and Character of the Chevalier John Paul Jones. City of Washington, 1825.

Date Due

NOV 2 2 1972			